The Andy Warhol Foundation for the Visual Arts 20-Year Report 1987–2007

65 Bleecker Street, 7th Floor
New York, NY 10012
telephone 212-387-7555
fax 212-387-7560
www.warholfoundation.org

ISBN 0-9765263-1-X

“Anybody can do

what
I
do."

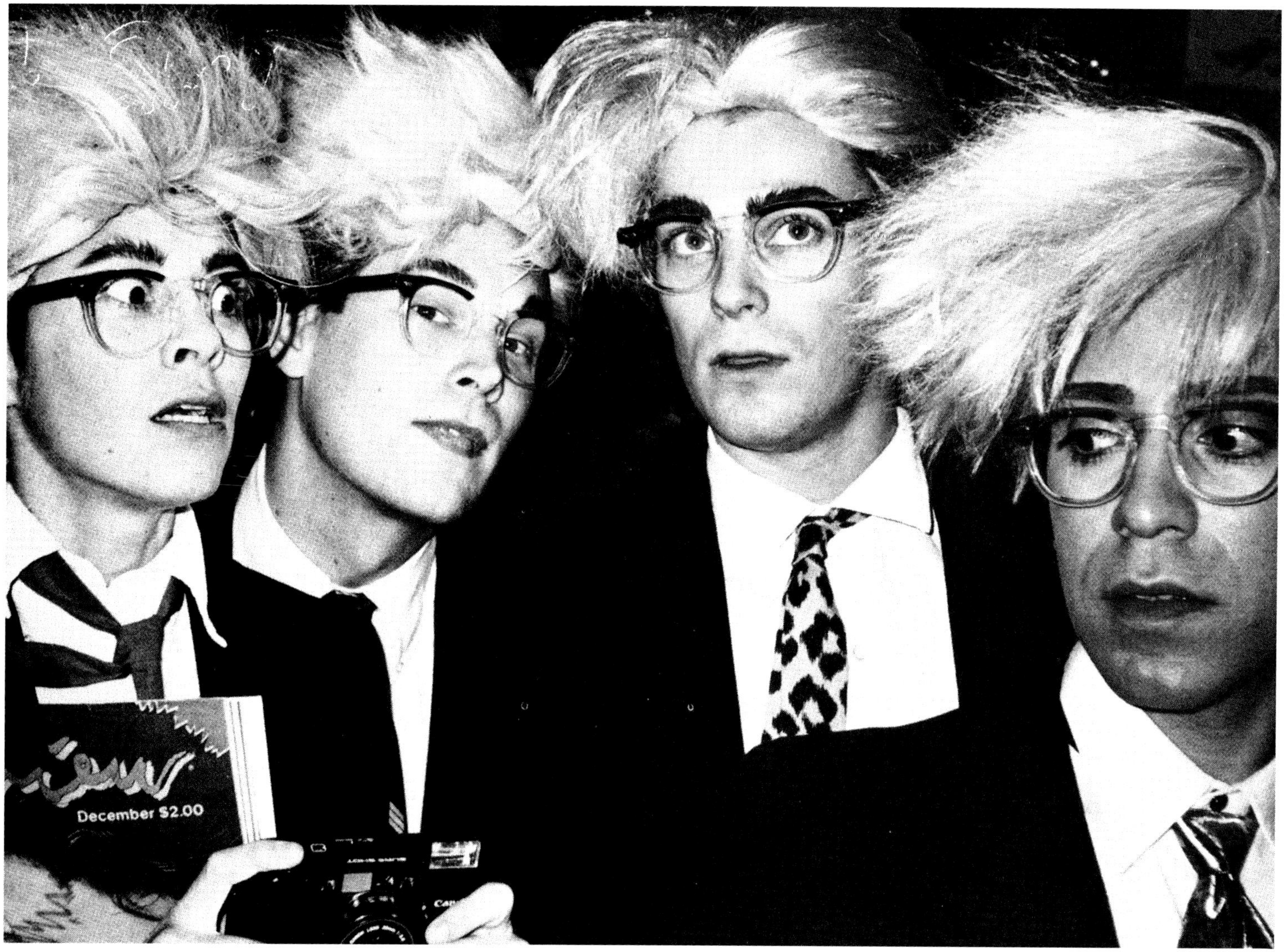

Four Men Wearing Andy Warhol Costumes, 1983, Gelatin silver print, 8 x 10 inches

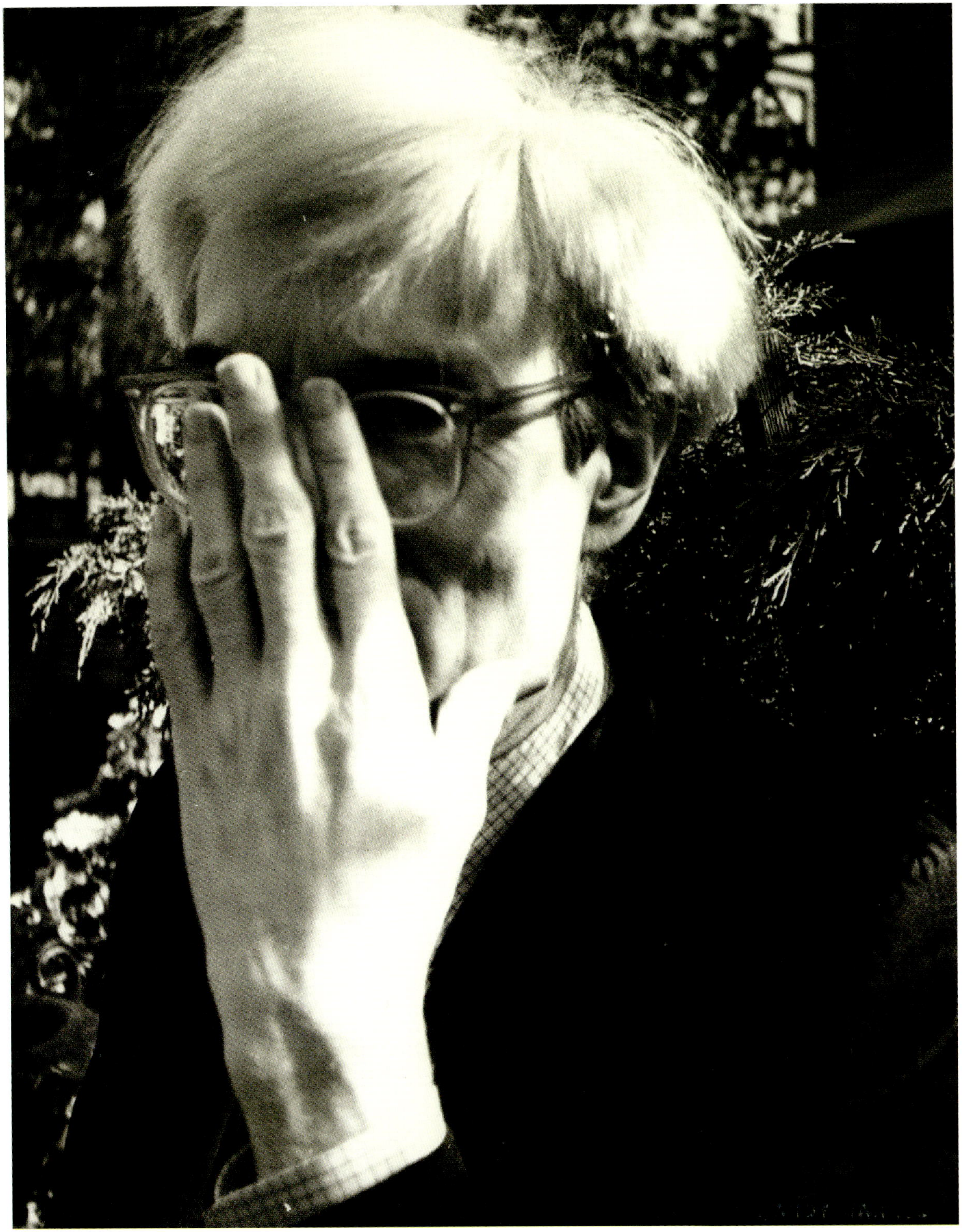

Andy Warhol, 1982, Gelatin silver print, 8 x 10 inches

Introduction

Andy Warhol's untimely death on February 22, 1987 was a shock to us all. Little did anyone imagine that when he entered the hospital for routine gallbladder surgery at the age of 58 he would never come out. That a figure whose prodigious creative output and seductively enigmatic public persona had secured him a central — even mythic — position in the public imagination should die such an avoidable, ignoble death seemed inconceivable. And yet it confirmed one of the most basic, inescapable truths about even the most celebrated among us: we are all mortal. Andy's death, a tragic loss to the art world and to the many other worlds with which his life and work were so inextricably intertwined, left a huge void for his friends and associates to grapple with. Luckily for all involved, however, Andy had prepared for this moment. In 1982 he had drafted a will providing for the creation, upon his death, of a charitable foundation dedicated to "the advancement of the visual arts". The foundation would be the primary beneficiary of his estate.

This gesture towards the unknown future proved to be one of the most consequential of his career. Founded with the fervor of grieving friends determined to enact Warhol's final wishes, The Andy Warhol Foundation for the Visual Arts has been keeping the memory of Warhol alive, enhancing his creative legacy and championing the significance of his work while advancing the entire field of contemporary art for the past twenty years. We are proud of what we have accomplished and think that Andy himself would be pleased with the strength, vitality and cultural impact of his foundation. This twenty-year report traces the major achievements of the foundation, which fall broadly into two categories: its ongoing efforts to secure Warhol's legacy and its role as the preeminent national funder of innovative contemporary art.

In helping to establish the comprehensive collection and study center of the Andy Warhol Museum in Pittsburgh, the foundation has paved the way for new Warhol scholarship and curatorial innovation as well as greater public understanding of Warhol's profound significance. Through cooperative exhibitions, loans and permanent placement of work in museums nationwide, the foundation has ensured that Warhol's vast and complex oeuvre is both widely accessible and properly cared for. Ongoing preservation and restoration of works in the foundation's care complement these efforts. The foundation's sustained support and oversight of thoroughly researched, extensively illustrated catalogues raisonné of Warhol's entire artistic output expand the possibilities for scholarship even further.

The foundation has used its ownership of the copyright to Warhol images as an opportunity to craft creative and responsible licensing policies that are friendly to scholars and artists wishing to use Warhol images for educational and creative purposes, and profitable to the foundation when the images are used for commercial purposes. Revenues from licensing agreements add significantly to those earned through the continued sale of work from the foundation's remaining art collection, enabling the foundation to build an endowment which now exceeds $240 million and from which it will make cash grants in excess of $11 million this year.

The primary focus of the foundation's grant making activity has been to support the creation, presentation and documentation of contemporary visual art, particularly work that is experimental, under-recognized, or challenging in nature. The program has been both pro-active in its approach to the field of cultural philanthropy and responsive to the changing needs of artists. A strong commitment to freedom of artistic expression led the foundation to play an active advocacy role for artists during the culture wars of the 1990s and continues to inform its support of organizations that fight censorship, protect artists' rights and defend their access to evolving technologies in the digital age.

Seeing the decline in national funding for individual artists in the late 1990s, the foundation helped establish — and now substantially supports — Creative Capital, an organization that directly addresses the needs of individual artists by awarding grants for innovative projects. The foundation's concern with the conditions affecting artists' lives has also inspired it to fund organizations which create artists' housing, provide access to affordable health care and offer legal assistance on behalf of artists.

In response to its recognition of a widespread need to stabilize small visual arts organizations, the foundation established the Warhol Initiative, a capacity-building program for non-profit visual arts organizations with budgets under $1 million. The recently launched Warhol Foundation Arts Writing Initiative is a similarly structured program aimed at strengthening the field of arts writing through grants to both arts writers and non-profit art journals.

Of special note in the foundation's history was its rapid response to the devastating events of both September 11, 2001 and hurricanes Katrina and Rita in summer 2005. Through the immediate authorization of crucial emergency relief grants targeted at affected artists and arts organizations, the Warhol board acted on the foundation's dearly held belief that arts and culture have a significant role to play in re-building communities in times of crisis.

Thanks to the leadership of our founding President, Archibald Gillies; past board chairs Brendan Gill and Wynn Kramarsky; a distinguished and diverse national board; and a talented and dedicated staff, the moral and financial fiber of the foundation is stronger than ever, enabling our programs and initiatives to evolve and expand to address the needs of the visual arts community nationwide. Twenty years after his death, Andy Warhol's impact on artists, art institutions and the creative culture of our country is stronger than ever, and in honor of our twentieth anniversary, we are proud to announce a new program that will extend his influence even further. Through the Andy Warhol Photographic Legacy Program, the foundation is donating over 28,500 unique Warhol photographs valued at more than $25 million to college and university art museums, galleries and collections throughout the United States.

Andy's desire to promote the "advancement of the visual arts" — and the realization of this desire by the foundation he created — have placed him, posthumously, at the helm of what is turning out to be a powerful new philanthropic movement among our nation's artists. We hope that Andy's example will serve as a role model for the increasing number of artists who wish to fortify the future of their field by helping other artists. Imagine how wonderful it will be when our nation, which has been so beleaguered by battles over public versus private funding for the arts, can look to this new and even more potent resource of artists supporting other artists. Toward this end, we at the Warhol Foundation will continue to devote our energy to expanding the depth and scope of our founder's support for artists and art institutions throughout the country. We encourage others to follow his visionary lead.

Joel Wachs, President
Sherri Geldin, Board Chair

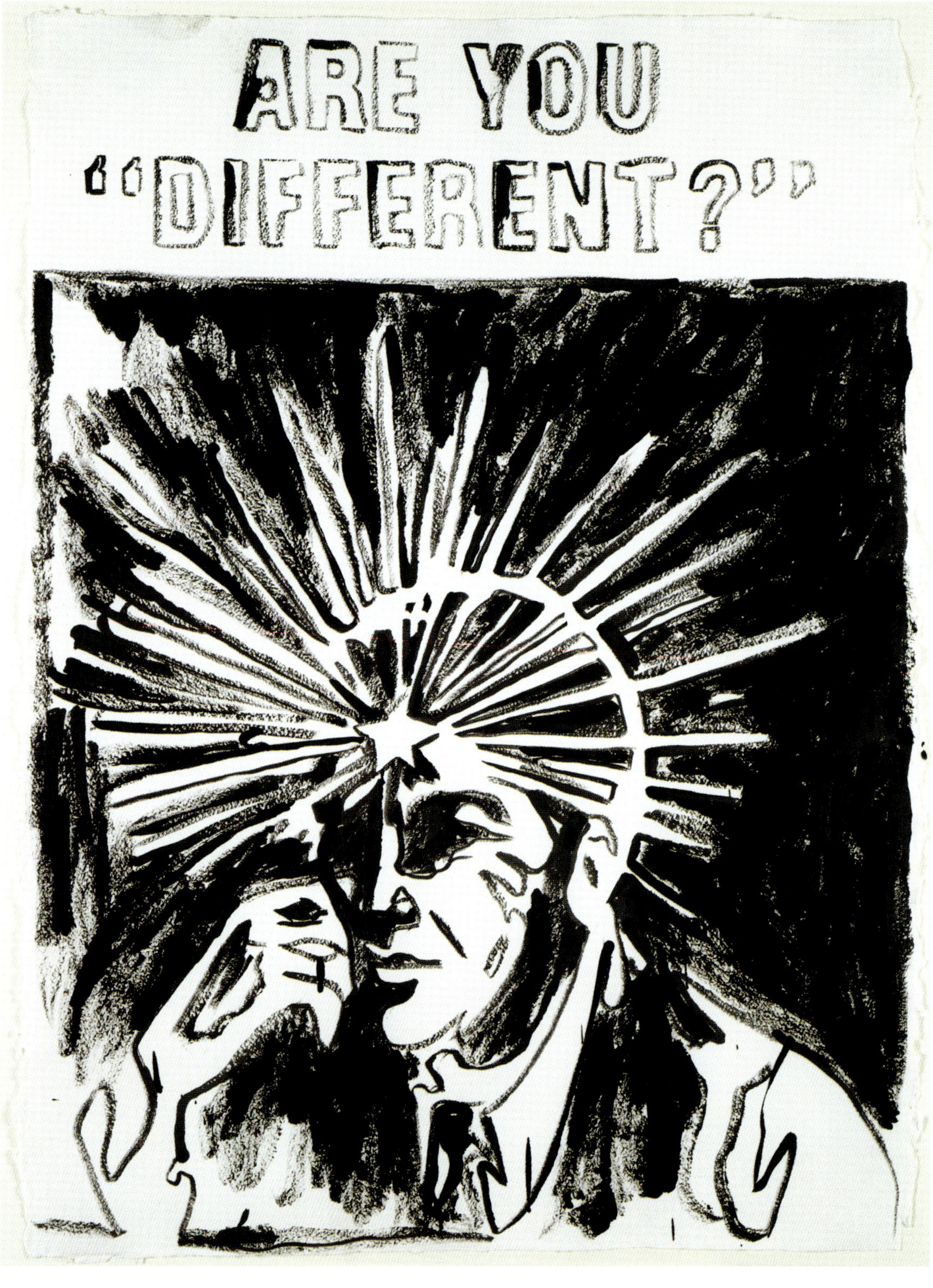

Are You "Different?", c.1985-86, Synthetic polymer paint on HMP paper, 31 1/8 x 23 1/2 inches

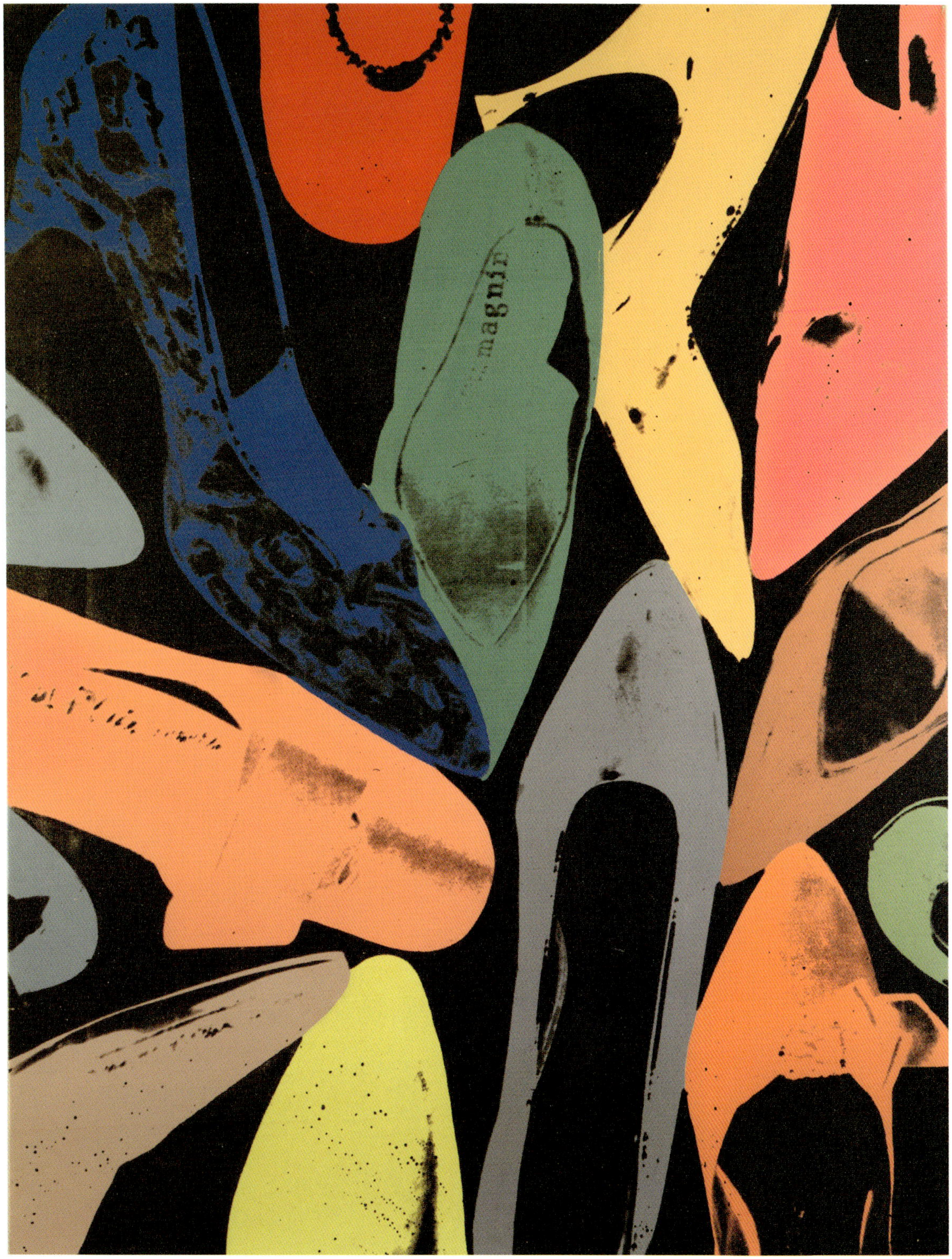

Diamond Dust Shoes, 1980, Synthetic polymer paint, diamond dust and silkscreen ink on canvas, 90 x 70 inches

“I never wanted to be a painter;

I wanted to be a tap-dancer."

The Program: Origins and Evolution

In the months after Andy Warhol's unexpected death, Frederick Hughes, the artist's business manager and executor; Vincent Fremont, Vice-President of Andy Warhol Enterprises, Inc.; and Andy's brother, John Warhola, began the effort to create the foundation which Warhol's will had mandated. Together they undertook extensive consultations with arts and philanthropic professionals on the design of the new organization, its goals, and its structure. The first question, it seemed, was what Warhol would have wanted; and in the will, the key phrase "the advancement of the visual arts" offered the best clue to his intentions.

"Advancement" suggested a foundation that would take a progressive, even visionary approach to the arts; contemporary art at its most forward-looking would be its sphere of action. The foundation's planners had to decide on many things, from the size of the board to the types of grantees to the structure of the staff, but their discussions had made one thing clear: the Warhol Foundation would follow the inventive, open-minded, experimental spirit of its founder. "The advancement of the visual arts" would be its guiding principle; supporting artists and progressive arts institutions would be at its heart.

Once the basic parameters of the organizational mission and structure had been put into place, the foundation decided to consult with the field to hear what its most urgent needs were and how Warhol's generosity could best serve them. In 1988, therefore, the fledgling foundation hosted a series of convenings. Artists, curators, administrators, educators, critics and others were brought together to offer their opinions on the role and function of the Warhol Foundation. The goal was to create a responsive, committed and engaged philanthropic organization that would have the needs and goals of its constituency — artists and the institutions that serve them — foremost in mind. Out of these discussions and their own internal deliberations, the foundation's leaders began to put in place the new foundation's program, with its aim of enabling cultural organizations and, through them, contemporary artists.

"We are grateful for the Foundation's support and for the opportunities for advancement it has afforded the Art Center. The center has grown exponentially on all fronts, exhibiting

Grantmaking

The program that emerged from the early discussions had a tripartite structure. Grants would be awarded in three areas: arts education, historic preservation, and curatorial — the program supporting the creation, presentation and documentation of contemporary art. In later years, the first two categories would gradually be phased out, leaving the foundation free to concentrate on the curatorial program. During its first decade, however, it made significant contributions to both arts education and historic preservation.

Arts Education and Historic Preservation

The foundation's arts education program sought to advance the visual arts by teaching young people to create and to appreciate art. A notable early project was a photography instruction program in the Durham, NC public schools led by artist Wendy Ewald; closer to home, the foundation funded the Studio in a School, which placed professional artists in New York City elementary schools. These projects, like others the foundation supported, had the merit of assisting contemporary artists in addition to their primary educational mission.

The foundation also incorporated its core values in its work in the field of historic preservation. A restoration of the Snow Clan House on the Hopi Reservation in Second Mesa, Arizona, was a community development project that trained tribe members in the construction and restoration techniques of their ancestors. A contribution to a major restoration of Fallingwater, the Frank Lloyd Wright house in western Pennsylvania, was a way for the foundation to support a masterwork of avant-garde architecture within the context of historic preservation.

Such projects suggest the value of the foundation's work in both arts education and historic preservation. Over time, however, the program evolved away from these two fields. In 1995, a study of the philanthropic landscape revealed that private funding for arts education was increasing, whereas that for contemporary art was stagnant or decreasing. The board concluded that the foundation's relatively limited resources would best serve the advancement of the visual arts when directly supporting the kinds of challenging, experimental contemporary art that had few other institutional funders. In 1995, arts education grants were phased out, while the last historic preservation grants were made in 1999.

Curatorial

The curatorial program has always been at the heart of the Warhol Foundation's mission. Over the years the foundation has supported museum exhibitions and catalogues, visual arts programming at smaller institutions, artist residencies and projects, arts publications, and public programming. It has always searched for projects that promise to be especially beneficial to artists, whether by providing needed exposure at important moments in their careers, or by giving them their first documentation, or simply by offering them an opportunity to create an important new piece.

Exhibitions

Throughout its twenty year history, the foundation has supported hundreds of contemporary art exhibitions, from retrospectives of high-profile artists at major institutions — those of Eva Hesse, David Hammons, Jack Smith and Bruce Nauman are good examples — to group shows of emerging artists at small venues in rural areas. While there is tremendous variety in the work the foundation has supported, certain themes emerge that give a picture of the foundation's concerns and interests over the years.

One of the most important of these is a commitment to the presentation of groundbreaking contemporary art that is supported by the strongest scholarship and documentation. An example is the 1996 exhibition *Inside the Visible* at the Institute of Contemporary Art, Boston. Curated by Catherine De Zegher, the show presented the work of 37 highly inventive women artists from three decades of the twentieth century: the 30s, the 60s and the 90s. It was accompanied by a film series which presented the work of such filmmakers as Maya Deren, Chantal Akerman and Yvonne Rainer. The catalogue, published by MIT Press, contained impressive scholarship by a number of writers including artists and critics Martha Rosler, Griselda Pollock, and Bracha Lichtenberg Ettinger, an artist and psychoanalyst.

A little over a decade later, in 2007, the Los Angeles Museum of Contemporary Art presented *WACK! Art and the Feminist Revolution*, a comprehensive survey of the international foundations and legacy of feminist art. With the work of over 120 artists,

greater confidence, stability and quality of programs. Your funding endorsement has been terrific, but it is the ripple effect for this organization, isolated in the reddest state in the curator Cornelia Butler's thoroughly researched exhibition expanded the boundaries of feminist art and presented new material for historical consideration at a time when many emerging artists, scholars, and curators are turning to feminist art as a generative movement in contemporary art history. Helen Molesworth, Catherine Lord and Abigail Solomon-Godeau, among others, contributed to the catalogue.

The foundation has a commitment to supporting exhibitions and organizations that present diverse and under-exposed artists. One such organization is the African Film Festival. Since 1993, it has shown the work of independent African filmmakers at the Film Society of Lincoln Center and the Brooklyn Museum of Art; a traveling component brings the films to numerous additional cities across the U.S. The festival gives exposure to African filmmakers who would otherwise be almost completely unknown in this country. In 2003, with funding from the foundation, the festival also published a comprehensive guide to African film that provided important documentation of this little-known body of work.

An exhibition that deserves special mention here is the 1992 show *Mining the Museum*, a breakout project for artist Fred Wilson. Organized by Lisa Corrin of The Contemporary Museum in Baltimore, and presented at the Maryland Historical Society, the show gave Wilson access to the society's permanent collection. Selecting artworks and artifacts from its storage rooms, he presented them in the museum's galleries, spotlighting peripheral figures in paintings and re-contextualizing objects and artworks so that they made visible an alternative American history. Seen from a new perspective, these objects told a tale in which slavery and racial oppression loomed large, and gave a different inflection to traditional understandings of the past.

Another more recent exhibition to tackle a hidden history was the North Dakota Museum of Art's *The Disappeared*. Curated by Laurel Reuter in 2006, the exhibition revolved around artists' responses to the "disappearance" of intellectuals, political activists and religious dissenters during the military dictatorships of the 1950s-1980s in Latin America. The kidnapping, torture and death of tens of thousands of people, long a repressed topic in the countries involved and never before addressed in an American museum, was fearlessly taken up by 14 contemporary artists from seven countries in Central and South America. Their work, a viscerally and aesthetically powerful indictment of unspeakable state crimes, is also an important demonstration of artists' collective role in ending the silence surrounding these extreme cases of human rights violations.

Artist-Centered Organizations

In addition to supporting exhibitions at larger institutions, the Warhol foundation has always taken an interest in artist-centered organizations — generally small, regional groups that serve artists and their communities in many different ways. They present work, (often providing emerging artists with their first significant exposure), host residencies, offer studio or workshop space, present public programming, and provide other key services to artists. Most also have strong commitments to their local communities. Project Row Houses is a notable example.

Project Row Houses, a public art project located in the heart of an African-American community, has a special mandate to support artists creating work concerned with African-American culture and history and to connect this work with the revitalization of the community. In 1992, artist Rick Lowe spotted a group of abandoned shotgun houses in a poor Houston neighborhood. He raised the funds to acquire and restore them, and ten of the twenty-two buildings are now dedicated to art, photography, and literary projects, while seven others belong to The Young Mothers Residential Program which provides transitional housing and services for young mothers and their children.

Another small artist-centered organization with equally strong ties to its community is the Salt Lake City Art Center, which serves a strikingly different constituency in a different way. Located in a part of the country that is often quite socially and politically conservative, the Salt Lake City Art Center is a progressive arts organization whose mission is to present high quality contemporary art. Although its community may have some resistance to the questions and challenges raised by such work, the center has positioned itself as an ambassador for contemporary art within it. While it readily presents work with challenging content, it is also committed to programs that reach out solicitously to engage local audiences.

A different kind of artist-centered organization altogether is Los Angeles' quirky but ambitious Museum of Jurassic Technology. Located in a major city, the museum benefits from its large

country, that has perhaps been even more significant. The Board, the staff, our audiences and other donors acknowledged immediately the gravity of the "Warhol Foundation

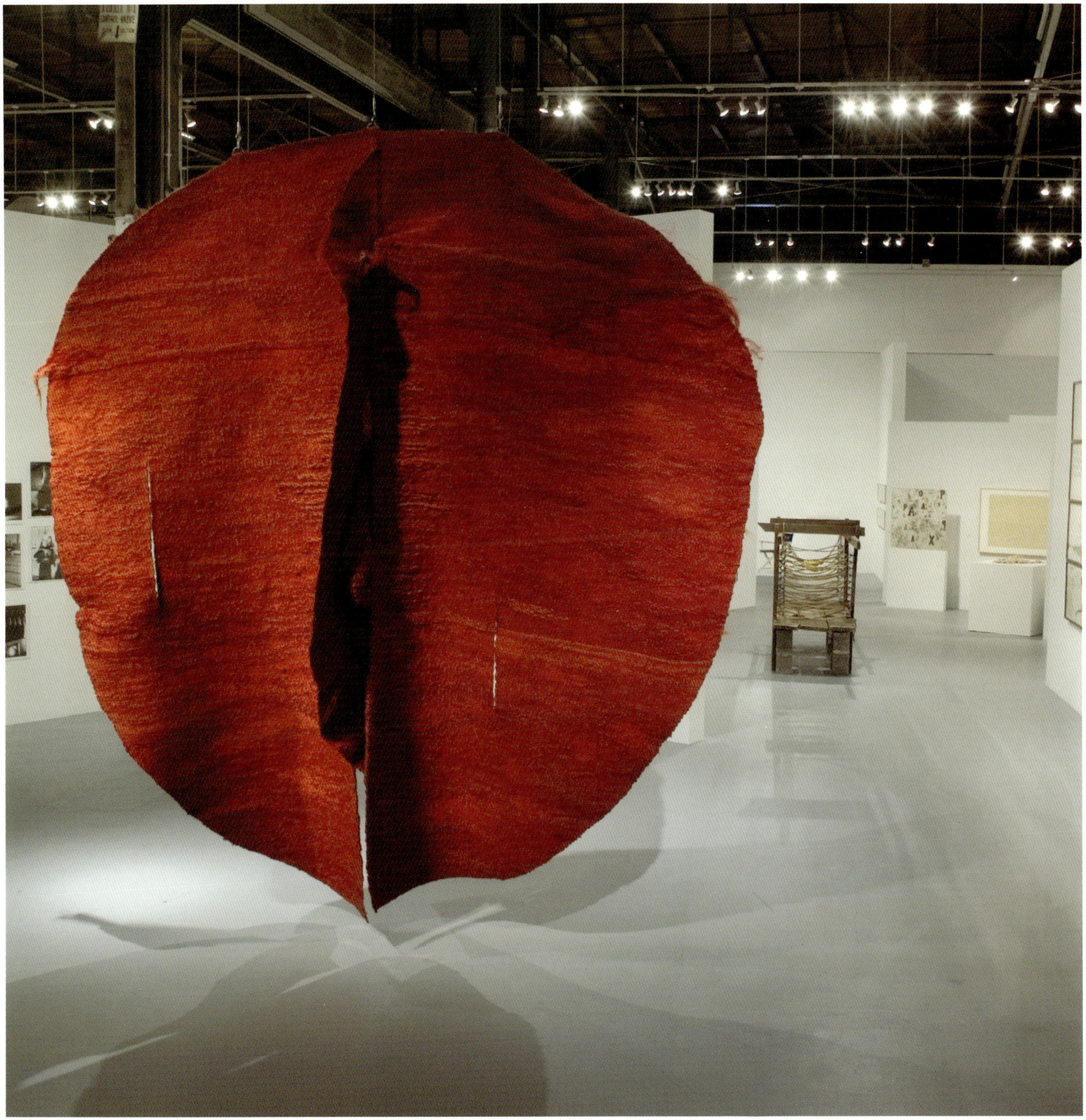

Installation view of *WACK! Art and the Feminist Revolution* at The Geffen Contemporary at MOCA, 2007

validation" and have given generously of time, money and commitment thanks to the leverage you provided." —*Salt Lake Art Center, Salt Lake City, UT*

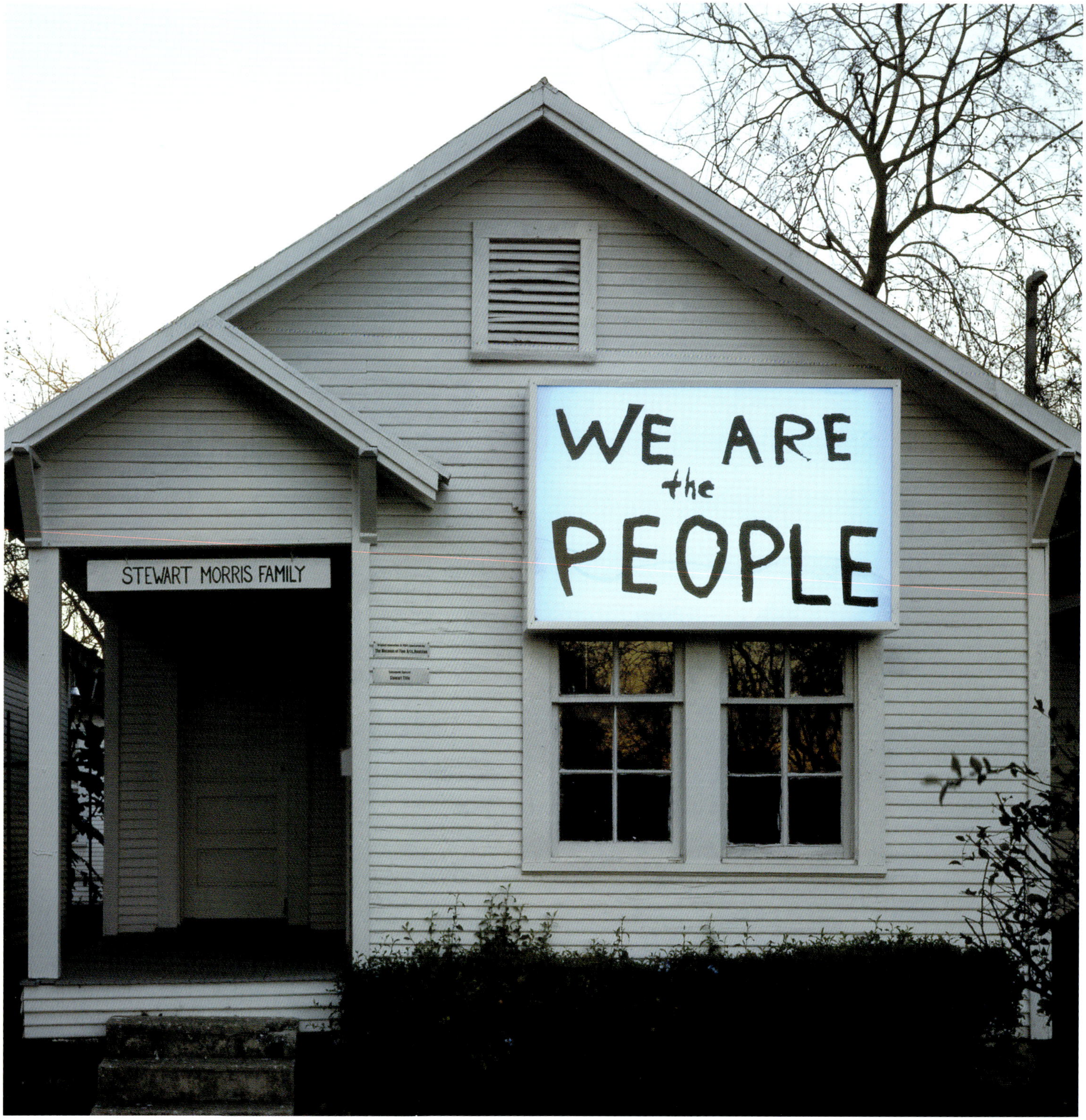

We Are the People**, Installation view of Sam Durant's project at Project Row Houses, Houston, TX**

"Through the Initiative program, our staff learned that we're not alone in supporting essential, non-commercial art and artists in a market-valued economy. More concretely, Out community of artists and culturally engaged public. Occupying a modest storefront on Venice Boulevard, it has a two-strand program: amassing a permanent collection of artworks, many of which are microscopic in scale and have been created using innovative technologies, and presenting artists who are little known due to the eccentric or marginalized nature of their work. The museum itself has been described as "a highly sophisticated and culturally significant work of contemporary art," but also as "a work of parody" deconstructing the semiotics of the modern museum. However it is understood, it is a unique institution whose charm and inherent creativity offer its visitors unusual experiences of aesthetic delight.

Media Organizations

The foundation has made many grants to media organizations. Appalshop, a community-based cultural center in Whitesburg, KY, in Appalachia, is one such group. It received funding for *Stranger with a Camera*, a film exploring the sometimes hostile relationship of local communities to the well-meaning outsiders who come to study and, at least in theory, help them. L.A. Freewaves, an innovative media arts magnet, has received funding for its video festivals, one in 1998, which presented artist-made videos at locations across Los Angeles, and another in 2006, by which time most of the work was presented to an international audience via the Internet. These two organizations, one deeply rooted in the traditions of Appalachia, the other at the cutting edge of global media art, represent two extremes of the range of important media organizations the foundation supports.

Artist Residencies

One of the most direct ways the foundation helps artists to further their careers and create new work is by funding residency programs. ArtPace, in downtown San Antonio, Texas, is an important example. Guest curators select nine artists a year to spend two months at its handsome 1920s facility. While there, they receive generous benefits, from housing and studio space to a sizable materials and travel budget and a stipend. The organization is notable for its ability to draw artists from all over the world while maintaining a strong commitment to those from its own region. Additional Warhol-funded organizations with outstanding residency programs are the Mattress Factory in Pittsburgh, and the Glassell School of Art in Houston, among many others.

Social Issues that Impact Artists

In addition to funding organizations that help advance artists' careers, the foundation also makes grants in areas that shape the conditions in which artists live and work. In recent years, the foundation has become increasingly concerned about two issues that have an especially powerful impact on artists: health care and housing. Because artists are often either self-employed or work only part-time or as freelancers, as a group they tend to be underinsured. Consequently, the foundation has provided significant funding to Working Today/The Freelancer's Union, a nonprofit organization that provides low-cost health insurance for independent workers, including artists. It also offers advocacy, information, networking services for independent workers, and an artist-outreach program. Another very promising project, this time in the area of artist housing, is one undertaken by Artspace Projects, a Minneapolis-based nonprofit real estate developer that specializes in low-cost housing developments for artists. Artspace has developed low-income live-work buildings for artists across the country; with the Warhol Foundation's assistance it is now taking on the challenge of creating such a project in New York City, one of the most competitive real estate markets in the country. As increasing numbers of artists are forced to leave New York due to its high cost of living, the prospect of new low-income housing and studio space for artists in the city is welcome indeed.

Creative Capital

One of the most significant ways in which the foundation has worked to provide support for artists is through Creative Capital. Creative Capital is an independent foundation housed in the Warhol offices that makes substantial grants directly to individual artists on a project basis. It began as an initiative of the Warhol Foundation in the wake of the termination by the National Endowment for the Arts of its individual grants program in the mid-1990s. Then foundation president Archibald Gillies enlisted other members of the philanthropic community in a major fund-raising effort to create an alternative source of direct funding for artists. The new organization would have as its mandate the cultivation of work that was experimental, innovative, or had challenging content. In 1999, with the participation of approximately twenty funders in addition to the Warhol Foundation, Creative Capital opened its doors.

North set up a server network and purchased critical equipment for our media program that has led to a growing audience for independent media. We have also completed a

As a national organization that funds artists working in all disciplines, Creative Capital honors the creative process with strategic interventions of financial support plus advisory services and promotional assistance at key moments in the development of an art project. This multi-faceted integrated system allows Creative Capital to build the capacity of the artist, with a funded project acting as a gateway into the artist's life.

To date, Creative Capital has supported 242 art projects with grants up to $50,000 and has worked with an additional 1,300 artists through its Professional Development Program, which delivers skill-building workshops on self-management to artists across the country. In addition to its initial $2 million grant and crucial support during Creative Capital's early years, the Warhol Foundation's recent ten-year, $10 million grant demonstrates its confidence in and commitment to Creative Capital's paradigm-shifting approach to serving artists.

Warhol Initiative

In today's environment, unfortunately, it is not only individual artists who have few sources of funding. As the foundation has discovered in its years of working closely with them, the small visual arts organizations that are so key to artists' well-being often struggle to survive. After a 1999 study commissioned by the foundation revealed that such organizations were chronically under-funded, with their sources of income dropping precipitously after the '90s culture wars, the foundation embarked on a new program to bolster organizational capacity among these groups. The Warhol Initiative offered selected small to mid-sized visual arts organizations large grants of approximately $125,000, along with professional consulting services. The goal was to help the groups gain a more stable financial footing and to improve their services to artists. Among the benefits provided were biennial conferences which brought the groups' leaders together for networking, workshops and training sessions with non-profit management consultants. After eight years of the ten-year $10 million initiative, the Warhol Initiative has served 58 visual arts organizations. Many of the grantees now have cash reserves that give them stability and much greater flexibility in their financial dealings; many have used the Initiative's resources to help them make important organizational transitions, such as moving to new facilities or enhancing their technology capabilities.

Arts Writing Initiative

The foundation recently turned its attention to another essential but under-funded area in the arts: criticism and general writing about the visual arts. In recent years, the art world has become truly globalized, so that arts journalists and critics must regularly undertake extensive travel and research in order to cover it properly. At the same time, pay for arts criticism, especially for work in periodicals, has remained shockingly low; often, there is little or no compensation for essays in catalogues or smaller journals. The foundation believes strongly that critical writing is an essential component of a thriving visual culture; it also is concerned that such work be accessible to a wide public while retaining intellectual rigor. With these ideas in mind, it designed the Warhol Foundation Arts Writing Initiative to encourage and reward distinguished writing about art. The program aims to strengthen the field as a whole and to highlight its significance in the cultural landscape.

The project has two components: grants to writers, which support various types of projects, from books to essays to experimental writing in new media; and grants to non-profit arts publications. The grants to individuals are made through Creative Capital, and follow its model of project-based grants augmented by individually tailored technical assistance and professional development services. Grants to art publications are administered by the foundation itself and offer capacity-building assistance to progressive, non-profit arts publications, including those representing unique regional, national or minority points of view. The grants seek to help these publications achieve greater financial stability, increase their audiences, and explore new forms of publishing, as well as new partnerships and distribution channels. Overall, the two strands of the Arts Writing Initiative have the goal of encouraging journals to take creative risks and to showcase ambitious, intellectually committed writing about art.

Emergency Grants

In the wake of two significant national crises, the terrorist attacks of September 11, 2001 and the devastation of the Gulf Coast by Hurricanes Katrina and Rita in summer 2005, the foundation reached out to offer general assistance grants to hard-hit arts organizations.

strategic plan and created operating reserves. Finally, we began preparations to build affordable artist housing / studios and finalized negotiations to purchase the 10,000-square

In September, 2001, in the days after the twin towers came down, the foundation gave a total of $100,000 to funds for police officers, firefighters, and emergency medical workers, and to the New York Times Neediest Cases Fund. It then began to consider how the event had affected local arts organizations. While only a few were physically affected (most notably the Lower Manhattan Cultural Council, whose World Trade Center offices were completely destroyed), many were hurt financially by the closure of the downtown area in the days after the attack and by the subsequent drop-off in visitors from outside the city, as well as by the diversion of charitable monies to the attack's direct victims. In December of that year, to help ameliorate the hardship they suffered, the foundation gave $700,000 in emergency grants to 32 downtown arts organizations.

After Hurricane Katrina, it was clear that Gulf Coast artists and arts organizations were, if anything, in worse shape than the New York City groups had been in 2001. The facilities of many had been damaged or destroyed, and the devastation of the region overall also meant that visitorship was likely to be minimal for the foreseeable future. In the winter of 2006, foundation staff made several trips to the region to meet with arts organizations there and assess their situations. Between January 2006 and April 2007, the foundation made grants totalling $1.85 million to Gulf Coast arts institutions. These funds were used to assist those that were recovering and rebuilding, and also to support organizations that were providing direct support to artists who had lost work, housing, studio space, and more. The emergency grants of 2001 and 2006 exemplify the foundation's commitment to its constituency and its readiness to take action outside its usual program to help organizations in crisis. As John Warhola remarked when the grants were authorized, "this is what Andy would have wanted."

Conclusion

Over the twenty years of the Warhol Foundation's history, it has carved out a niche for itself as a flexible and innovative supporter of contemporary art, both in this country and abroad. The foundation has displayed a willingness to fund controversial projects and to take on difficult political issues; it has also tried to construct its programs with a concerted attention to the needs and aims of the arts organizations it serves. As the discussion here has made clear, it funds a wide range of projects and organizations within the field of the visual arts, and believes as much in the value of small community arts organizations as it does in high-profile national institutions. In the future, the foundation hopes to broaden its grantmaking scope while continuing to provide millions of dollars in support to artists and arts organizations. A glance at a few of the most recent grants gives a good indication of the range of the foundation's priorities and future interests: n.paradoxa, a feminist art journal; a festival of films from Middle Eastern countries; a residency in Trinidad for artists of the Caribbean diaspora; a film project about the history of ACT UP; a study of artist-endowed foundations; and exhibitions of artists Lynne Hershman Leeson, Kim Jones, Allan Kaprow, Huang Yong Ping, Kara Walker and Gordon Matta-Clark. The foundation is proud of the role it has played in the art world over the past two decades, because it has helped many artists and arts organizations while keeping faith with the adventurous, unconventional spirit of Andy Warhol, the great artist who was its founder and benefactor.

foot facility we have leased from the local government for 13 years." —*Out North, Anchorage, AK*

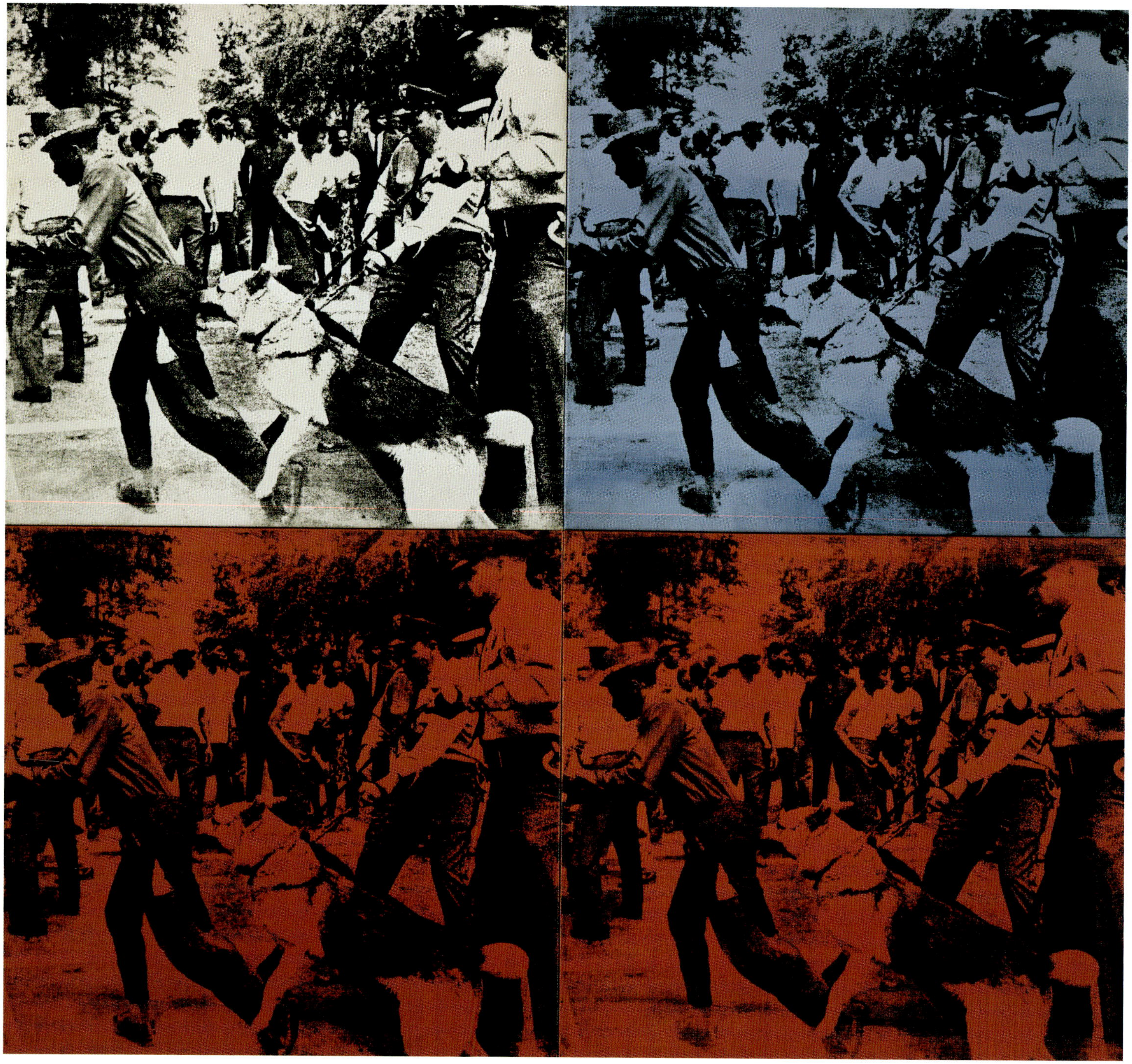

Little Race Riot, 1964, Silkscreen ink on synthetic polymer paint on canvas, 30 x 33 inches

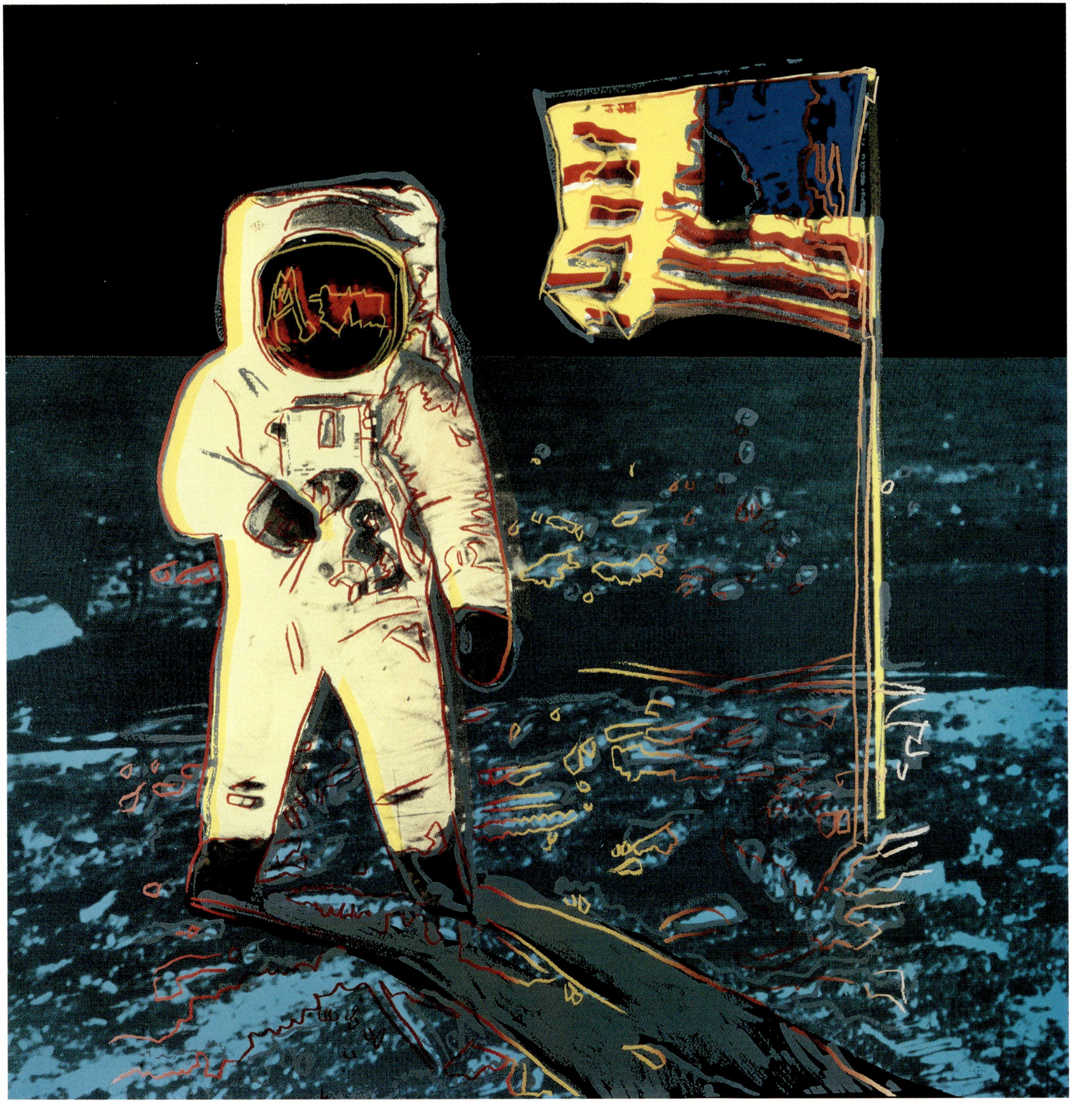

Moonwalk, 1987, Screen-print on Lenox Museum Board, 38 x 38 inches

“They always say time changes things,

but you actually have to change them yourself."

Freedom of Expression

The Warhol Foundation strongly believes that the arts are an essential part of an open, enlightened democracy and that freedom of artistic expression is fundamental to the health of our culture. Both because its founding coincided with some of the fiercest battles of the culture wars and because Warhol himself embraced work with sensitive or controversial content, defending the First Amendment rights of artists and the organizations that support them has been at the heart of the foundation's activities for twenty years.

Financial Support

To begin with, the foundation has not hesitated to fund artwork and exhibitions with potentially controversial sexual, political or religious content through its regular program grants. To cite just two of many examples, a 1999 retrospective of David Wojnarowicz at the New Museum presented work with both sexual and violent content and addressed the politically charged topic of AIDS head-on. A 2006 exhibition and catalogue *Harmful: the Art of American Censorship* at Georgia State University brought together works that had generated tremendous controversy — Andreas Serrano's *Piss Christ* and pieces by Karen Finley and Robert Mapplethorpe among others — in a show at a publicly funded institution in the South. The exhibition was accompanied by extensive public programming that aimed to provoke an open and constructive dialogue about art, politics and censorship in America.

Such controversies about artistic content and government funding, however, are hardly limited to this country; in 2005, the foundation provided critical funding for *The Eighth Square*, a show about gender politics and marginalized sexuality at the Museum Ludwig in Cologne, Germany, when its state funding was rescinded because of controversial content. In all of these cases, the foundation's strong commitment to freedom of artistic expression caused it to step forward to support work that had been censored for being unseemly or immoral.

But the foundation believes that in order to fight effectively against the censorship of art, whether direct (removing work from gallery walls) or indirect (cutting off funding), supporting controversial exhibitions is not enough. So it has consistently made grants for legal and other advocacy work that defends artists and arts institutions from attempted censorship. Perhaps the

"As we remain true to our core mission....we have been working to expand the educational component of our work so as to widen the constituency committed to defending free highest-profile example of this was the Brooklyn Museum of Art controversy. In 1999, New York Mayor Rudolph Giuliani, outraged by British artist Chris Offili's painting of the Virgin Mary that was decorated with elephant dung, threatened to cut off all city funding to the museum if it did not remove the picture from the exhibition. The $7 million amounted to a third of the museum's budget; its withdrawal would have caused the entire institution to shut down. The foundation responded to the crisis immediately with support for the lawsuit, ultimately victorious, that the museum brought against the city.

The foundation has also funded the American Civil Liberties Union's art censorship project, which provides advocacy and litigation services to artists and arts institutions threatened with censorship, and the National Coalition Against Censorship, an advocacy group that educates and provides resources to artists and the general public on freedom of expression issues. In recent years, the foundation has also extended its efforts to the digital realm, funding Public Knowledge, a digital rights advocacy group that disseminates information about censorship, copyright law, and other issues specific to Internet-based expression.

Public Events

In May 1993 the Warhol Foundation, along with the Robert Sterling Clark Foundation, the Nathan Cummings Foundation, the Joyce Mertz-Gilmore Foundation and the Rockefeller Foundation co-sponsored a public event at the Museum of Modern Art in New York in support of artists and presenters then being charged with indecency. Guest speakers, performance artist Laurie Anderson, choreographer-dancer Bill T. Jones, *New York Times* columnist Anthony Lewis, and New York Shakespeare Festival producer George C. Wolfe laid out in dramatic ways the positive necessity for speaking out and taking action. Citations were presented to 16 individuals who had made unusual contributions to upholding the constitutional principle of freedom of expression.

Arts, Culture and Society

Between 1994 and 2002 the foundation published twelve papers through its Arts, Culture and Society program to foster public debate about the global economic and societal forces affecting the arts:

A Global Culture? by author David Rieff

Global Culture and the American Cosmos by historical sociologist Orlando Patterson

Between a Rock and a Hard Place by critic, artist and curator Robert Storr

Resisting the Dangerous Journey: The Crisis of Journalistic Criticism and *Convenience and Process: Private versus Public Arts Funding* by critic, teacher and curator Michael Brenson

Coming of Age with the Muses: Change in the Age of Multiculturalism by Susana Torruella Leval, Director Emerita, El Museo del Barrio

A Democracy of Voices: Free Expression in the U.S. by journalist Nan Levinson

INDECENCY: The Ongoing American Debate Over Sex, Children, Free Speech, and Dirty Words by lawyer and author Marjorie Heins

Created Commons by author Lewis Hyde

A New Commitment: To Artists, Creativity, and Freedom of Expression in the 21st Century by former Warhol Foundation President, Archibald Gillies

The 1960s in Bamako: Malick Sidibé and James Brown by author and filmmaker Manthia Diawara

Where the Green Ants Dream: Aspects of Community in Six Parts by artist and art historian Carol Becker

In a related project, the foundation commissioned a cross-disciplinary study by cultural geographer Marie Cieri and Durfee Foundation Director Claire Peeps that culminated in the 2000 publication of *Activists Speak Out*. Through a series of interviews with activists in civil rights, gay and lesbian rights, the environment, women's issues, health, youth, education, labor and the arts, the book addresses the role activists can play in teaching artists how to build community in the face of political adversity.

Wynn Kramarsky Freedom of Artistic Expression Grant

To recognize the work of organizations with a deep-seated commitment to preserving and defending the First Amendment rights of artists, the foundation inaugurated the annual Wynn Kramarsky Freedom of Artistic Expression Grant in 2006. Created in honor of the foundation's former Board Chair, the grant rewards outstanding advocacy, legal, and curatorial efforts on behalf of those whose rights to free expression have been challenged.

speech. For this opportunity we are greatly indebted to the support of the Andy Warhol Foundation." —*National Coalition Against Censorship, New York*

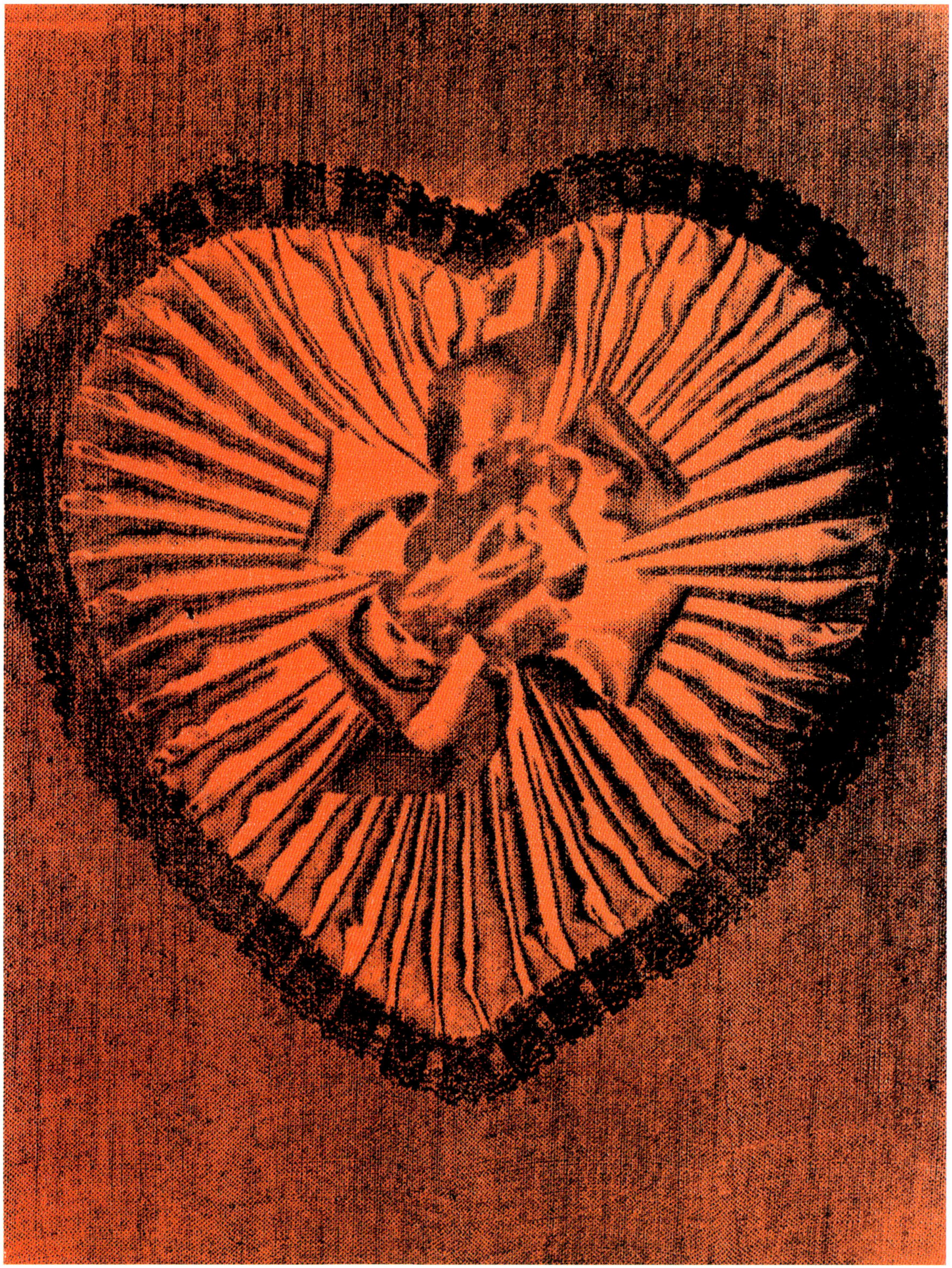

Heart with Bow, 1983, Synthetic polymer paint and silkscreen ink on canvas, 14 x 11 inches

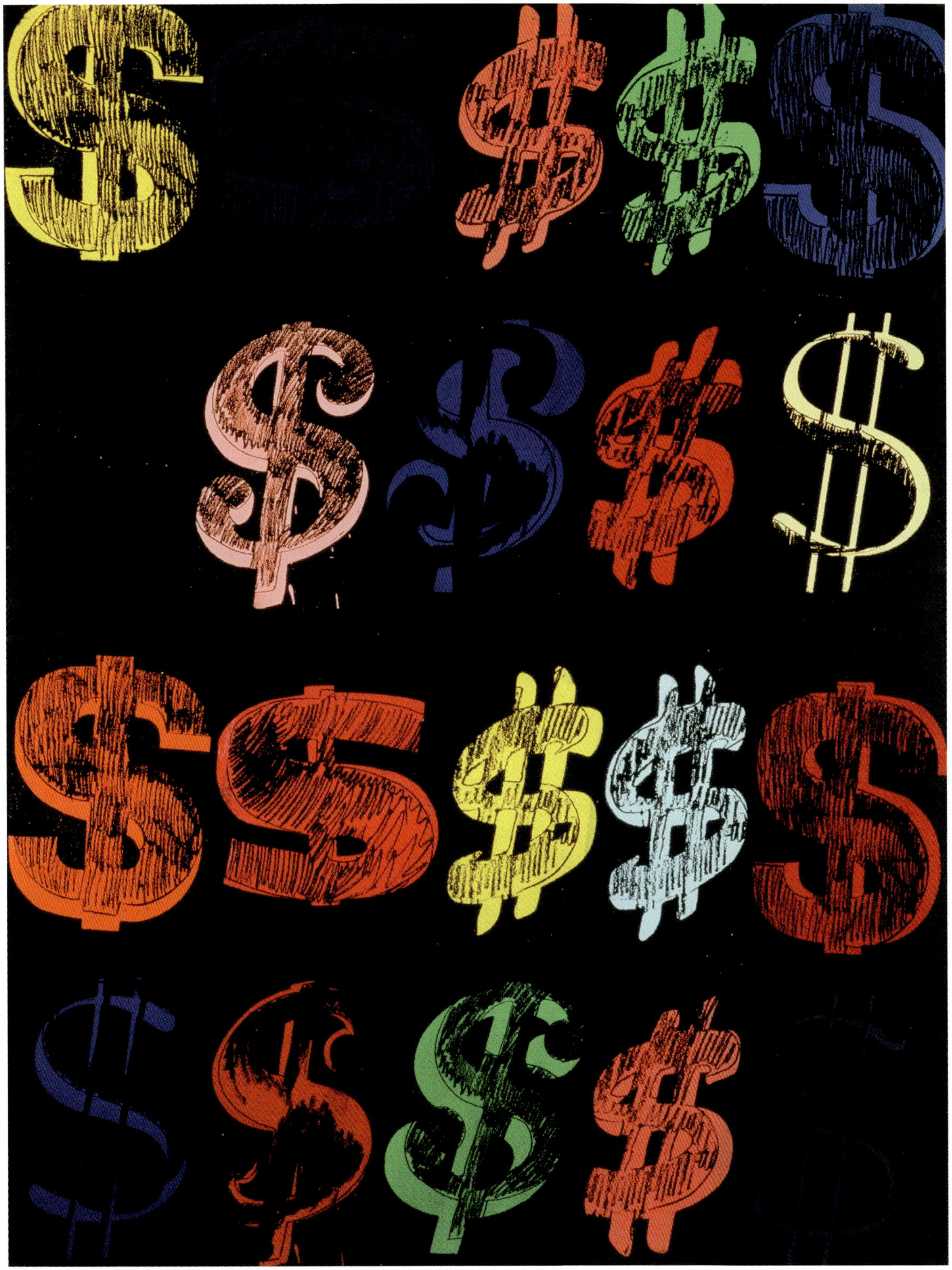

Dollar Signs, 1981, Synthetic polymer paint and silkscreen ink on canvas, 90 x 70 inches

“‘Well, what do you love most?’

That's how I started painting money."

Exhibitions

Since its incorporation in 1987, one of the foundation's most important priorities has been to present Warhol's work to the public in a scholarly and focused manner. To this end, the foundation has loaned a total of approximately 11,000 works from its extraordinarily diverse collection to 221 exhibitions worldwide. These works include paintings, sculptures, drawings, photography and prints from the early 1950s through the 1980s.

In the years shortly after Warhol's death, several large-scale exhibitions laid the groundwork for the many inventive curatorial approaches and exhibition strategies that would evolve in subsequent years. The first comprehensive critical examination of Warhol's artistic career, *Andy Warhol: A Retrospective*, was held in 1989 at the Museum of Modern Art, New York and traveled to five other national and international venues. It included approximately 300 paintings, drawings, sculptures, photographs and films drawn from public and private collections. The exhibition began with work of the 1950s and an early series of hand-painted images based on advertisements and comic strips from the 1960s, and concluded with the *Last Supper* paintings and the *Camouflage* works, executed just before his death in February 1987.

Inspired by interest from the Narodni Galeri in Prague, which wished to exhibit works by Warhol in Czechoslovakia — the land of his ancestors — The Museum of Modern Art also organized *The Prints of Andy Warhol*, a landmark exhibition that traveled to six international venues including five museums in Eastern Europe in 1990. The survey spanned Warhol's entire printmaking career and included his first published print, *Cooking Pot* (1962) and one of his last published portfolios, *Moonwalk*, from 1987.

A pioneering exhibition of Warhol's early work entitled *Success is a Job in New York: The Early Art and Business of Andy Warhol* was held at the Grey Art Gallery and Study Center, New York University in 1989 and traveled to five additional national and international venues. The exhibition focused on Warhol's early commercial work including the promotionals that he sent to the clients for whom he worked as an illustrator. *A is an Alphabet* (1953), a portfolio of twenty-six prints based on blotted line drawings, was one such project; *Wild Raspberries* (1959), a cookbook for which Warhol's collaborator, Suzy Frankfurt, wrote the recipes and Warhol provided the sly, whimsical illustrations was

"With the generous support of the Andy Warhol Foundation for the Visual Arts, the University of Michigan Museum of Art produced *Betye Saar: Extending the Frozen Moment*....

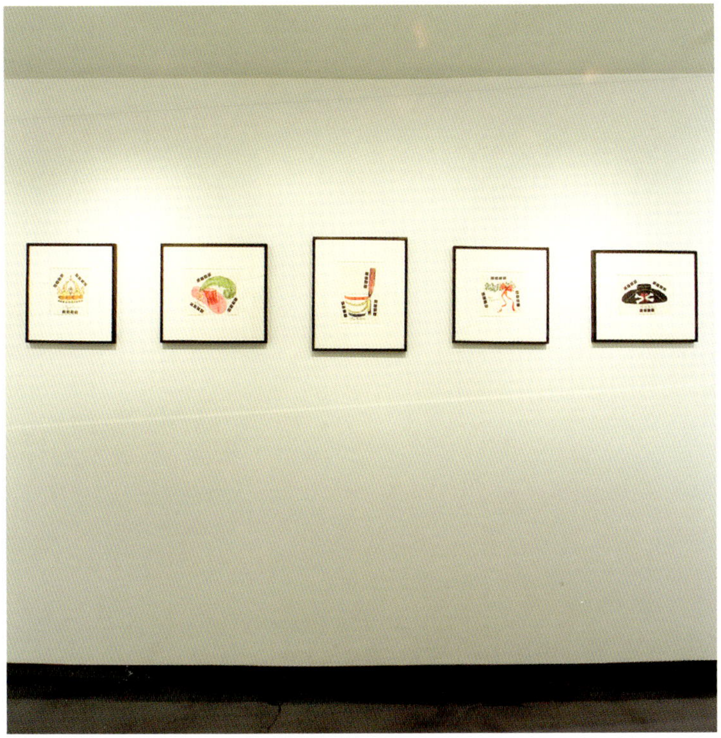

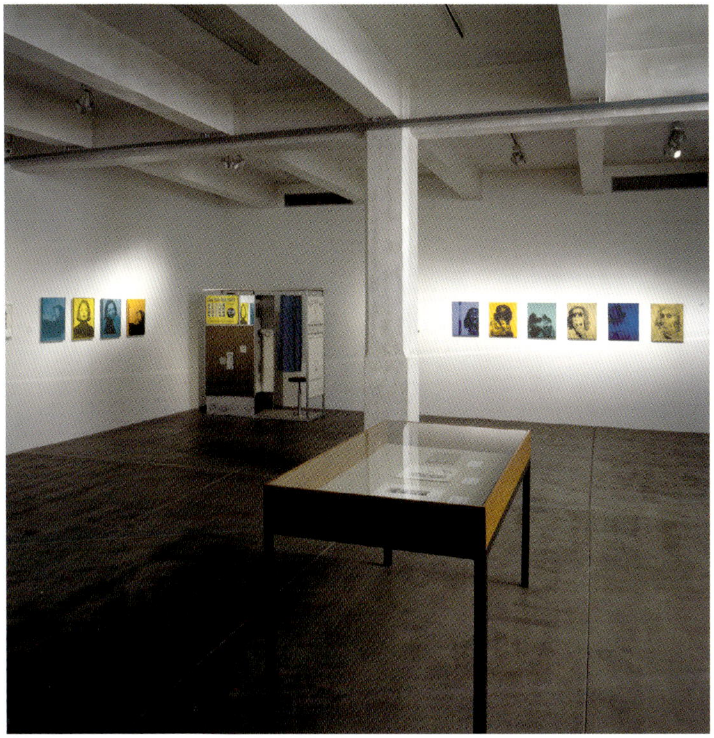

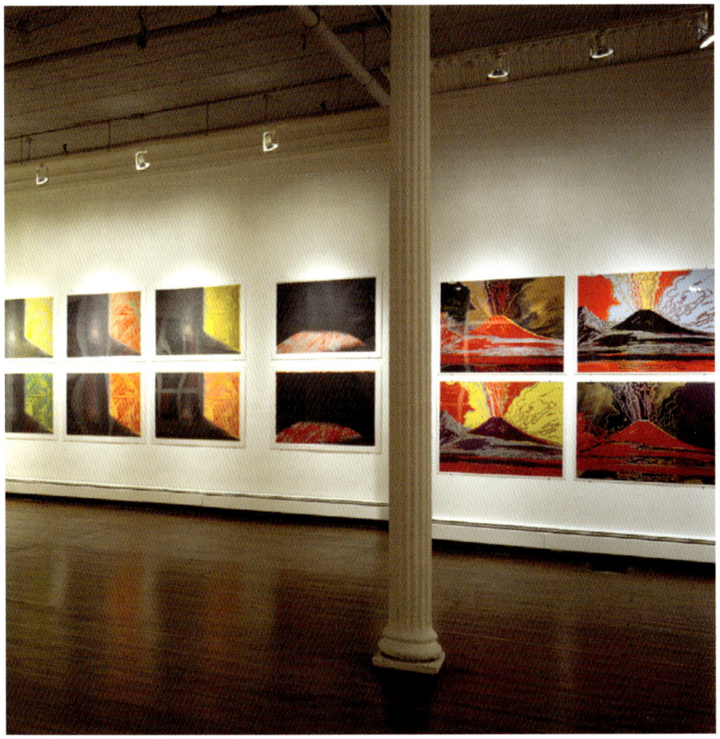

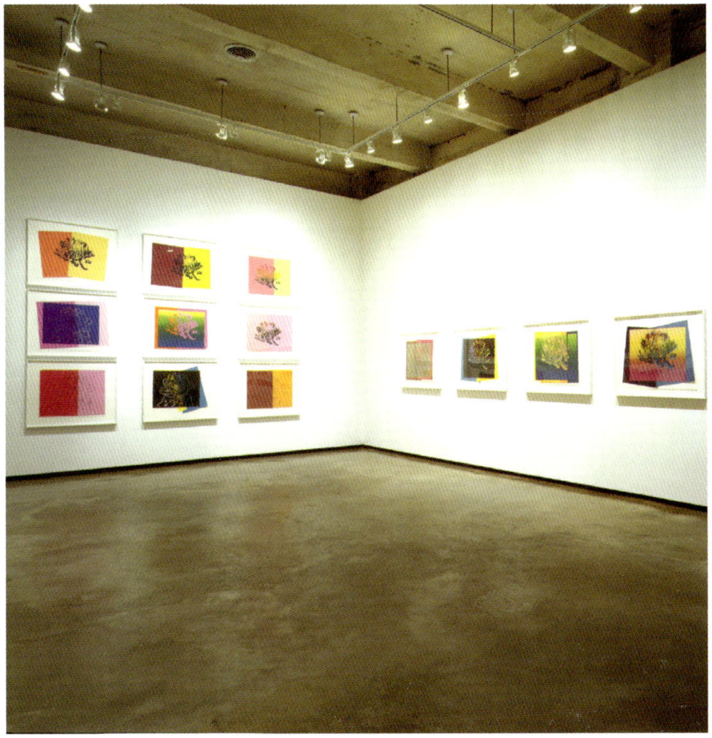

upper left: ***Andy Warhol's Hats*****, Paul Kasmin Gallery, New York, October 11 – November 11, 2006;** upper right: ***Andy Warhol – Photography*** **at The Andy Warhol Museum, Pittsburgh, November 6, 1999 – January 30, 2000;** lower left: ***Unique Screenprints Part I, 1967–1987*****, Ronald Feldman Fine Arts, New York, January 10 – February 7, 1998;** lower right: ***Andy Warhol Kiku*****, Paul Kasmin Gallery, New York, March 18 – April 17, 2006**

Your grant offered potential funders and venues critical evidence of the project's quality...The national tour now includes the Norton Museum in West Palm Beach, the Pennsylvania

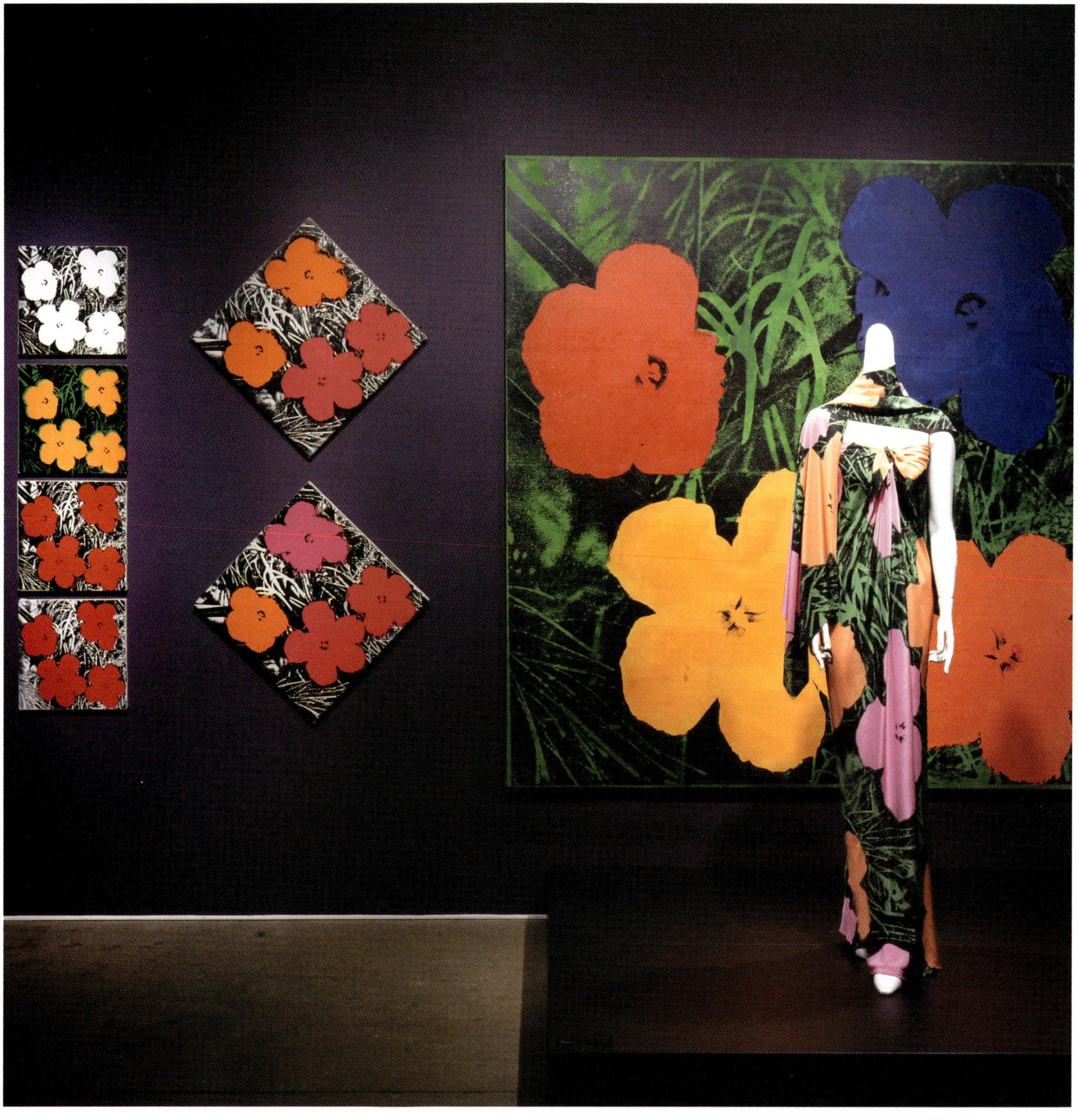

Andy Warhol's *Flowers* and Halston dress, *The Warhol Look: Glamour Style Fashion* at The Andy Warhol Museum, 2000

Academy of the Fine Arts in Philadelphia, and the Crocker Art Museum in Sacramento. One recent comment book entry noted, 'This is the most important, powerful, inspiring another. More personal works such as gold shoe collages, each depicting a particular famous personality, were shown too, as were numerous sketchbooks containing ballpoint pen drawings of men's feet.

Another early exhibition, *Andy Warhol Photobooth Pictures*, at the Robert Miller Gallery (1989), presented Warhol's four-frame vertical photographic portrait strips of friends, colleagues, commissioned sitters and himself. Taken in automated photobooth machines predominantly in the 1960s, these works formed the basis of many of Warhol's paintings and drawings.

In the years following these initial shows, Warhol exhibitions became smaller and more specialized, focusing on particular aspects of his career. Some were organized by subject, such as *Andy Warhol: The Last Supper Paintings* at Dia Center for the Arts (1995) and *Andy Warhol Nudes* at Robert Miller Gallery, New York (1995); and others by medium, such as *Andy Warhol: Drawings 1952–1986* at Galerie Thaddeus Ropac, Paris and Salzburg (1994) and *Andy Warhol: Gold, Silver & Other Early Drawings* at Anthony d'Offay Gallery, London (1994).

One of these specialized exhibitions was significantly larger than the others in scale because the work it focused on — portraits — played such a central role in Warhol's career. *Andy Warhol Portraits of the Seventies and Eighties* traveled internationally to five venues beginning at the Museum of Contemporary Art, Sydney (1993) and concluding at the Achenbach Kunsthandel, Düsseldorf (1995). In the portraits featured in this exhibition, Warhol documented the world around him with sitters ranging from glamorous rock star celebrities like Mick Jagger, John Lennon and Grace Jones to artists such as Joseph Beuys, Georgia O'Keeffe and Gilbert & George.

In 1994 the Kunsthalle Basel organized the exhibition *Andy Warhol: Abstract*, which examined six different painting series created by Warhol between 1977 and 1986. The *Oxidations, Shadows, Eggs, Yarns, Rorschachs* and *Camouflages* were all relatively unknown at the time of the exhibition and were considered unusual for Warhol since they were not based on photographs of personalities, products or events but rather on the process of painting itself. After that exhibition, several others including *Andy Warhol Rorschach Paintings* at Gagosian Gallery, New York (1996), *Eggs by Andy Warhol* at Jablonka Galerie,

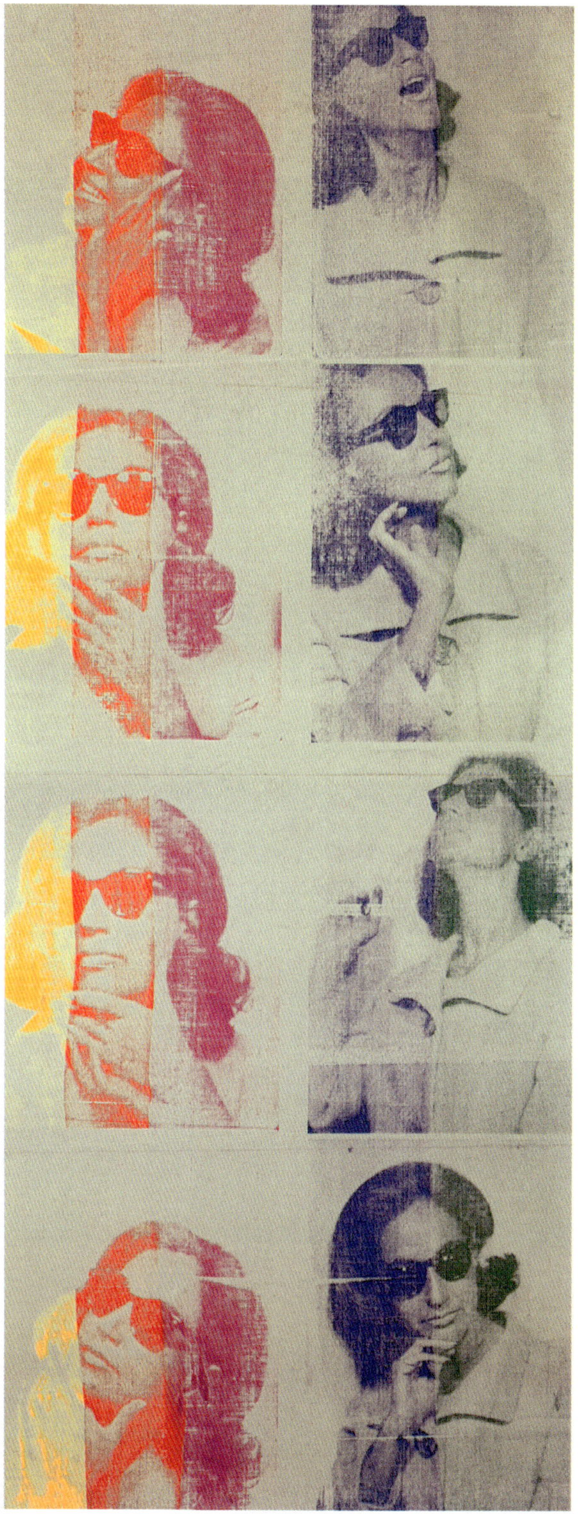

***Ethel Scull*, 1963, Synthetic polymer paint and silkscreen ink on canvas, 83 x 36 inches**

exhibit I have ever seen here or anywhere. Thank you for bringing it to Ann Arbor.'" —*University of Michigan Museum of Art, Ann Arbor, MI*

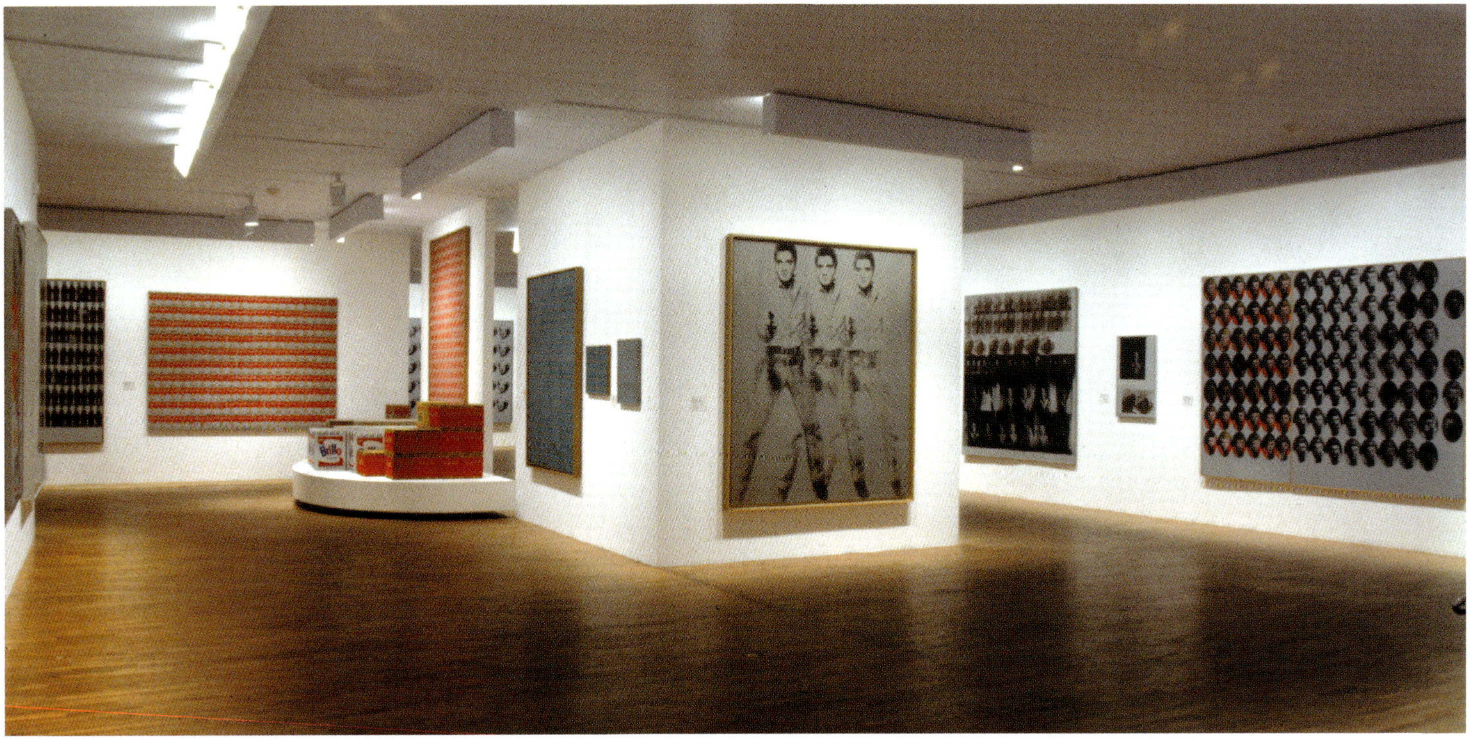

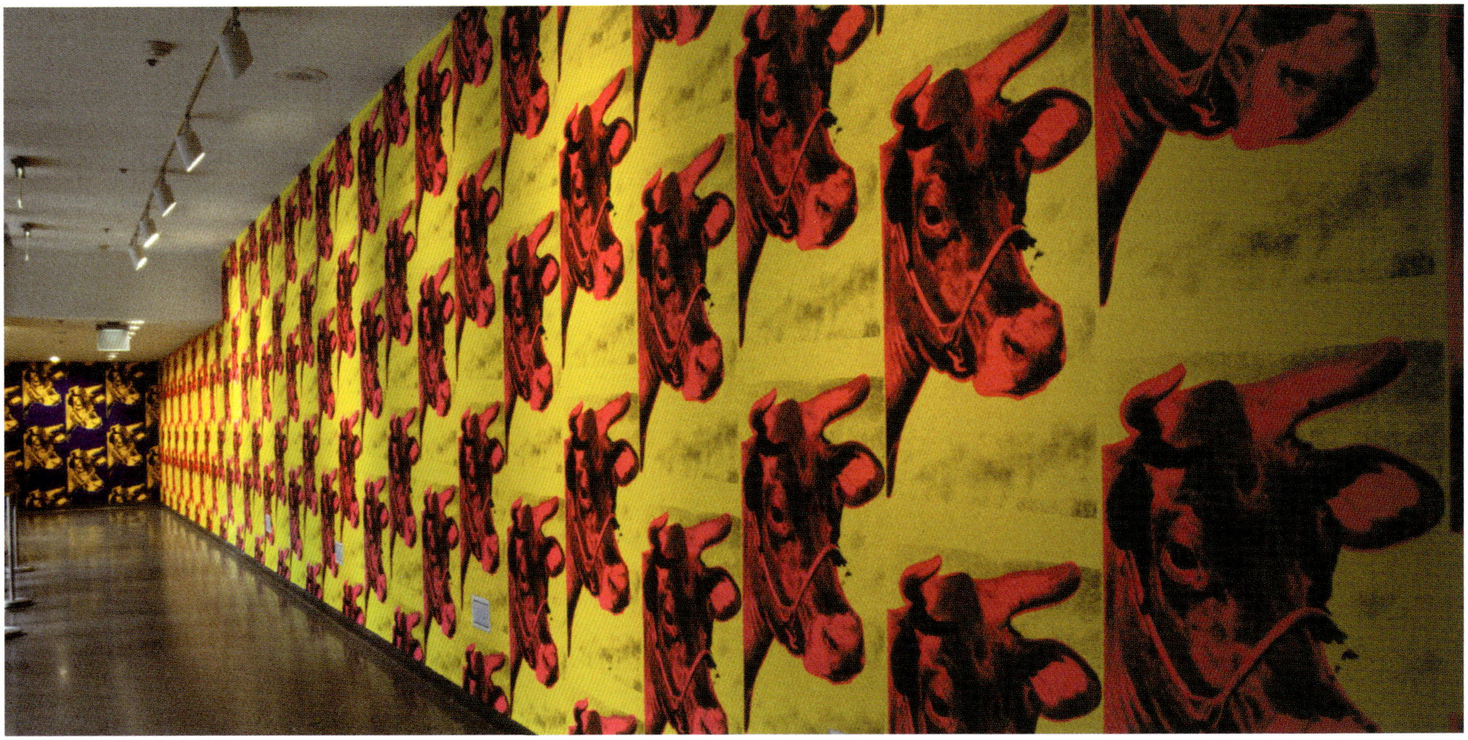

Installation views of the exhibition *Andy Warhol: A Retrospective* at The Museum of Modern Art, New York, February 6, 1989 – May 2, 1989

"...Pablo Picasso once said, 'Art washes away from the soul the dust of everyday life.' Since hurricane Katrina, there has been an abundance of 'dust' that has covered all of us.

Cologne (1997) and *Andy Warhol Oxidation Paintings* at Galerie Daniel Blau, Munich (1998) continued to explore Warhol's interest in abstraction.

With the exception of two early photography exhibitions, *Andy Warhol Photobooth Pictures* at the Robert Miller Gallery in New York (1989) and *Andy Warhol Polaroids 1971–1986* at the Pace/MacGill Gallery in New York (1992), Warhol's black and white photographs, polaroids and sewn photographs were not widely seen in the 1990s. In 1999, however, the Hamburger Kunsthalle and the Andy Warhol Museum organized *Andy Warhol Photography*, a thorough examination of Warhol's photographic practice, which traveled to the International Center of Photography, New York. In the same year, *NadarWarhol: ParisNew York*, an exhibition organized by the J. Paul Getty Museum in Los Angeles, explored the similarities between Warhol's photographs and the work of 19th century Parisian photographer Nadar, looking specifically at the role of the visual artist in relation to celebrity and fame. Also in 1999, the Galleria Lawrence Rubin, Milan presented an exhibition of Warhol's stitched photographs, the unusual format he developed in the early 1980s in which identical images were sewn together with thread into serial works.

These three exhibitions inaugurated a proliferation of Warhol photography exhibitions worldwide. In 2001, *Andy Warhol's Visual Memory* (Galerie Bruno Bischofberger, Zürich) presented black and white photographs taken by Warhol between 1976 and 1987. The exhibition demonstrated Warhol's interest in all facets of contemporary life and included works as diverse as a serial composition of stacked jars of Hellmann's mayonnaise, a portrait of the writer Truman Capote and an interior view of a hair salon. The 2006 exhibition *Warhol's World* at Hauser & Wirth, London, and Zwirner & Wirth, New York presented photographs documenting Warhol's New York social scene at Studio 54 and his life at the Factory.

Andy Warhol — The Late Work, organized in 2004 by Museum Kunst Palast, Düsseldorf, was an in-depth examination of the last fifteen years of Warhol's career which presented films, videos and painting series from the 1970s and 1980s (*Mao, Skulls, Reversals and Retrospectives* and *The Last Supper*). It was also one of the first exhibitions to devote significant attention to Warhol's contact sheets. Approximately eighty contact sheets were paired with extracts from Andy Warhol's *Diaries*. These texts, in combination with the marks and notes made directly on the contact sheets with colored wax crayons, provided information about how Warhol selected images and gave viewers insight into his working process.

Other views into Warhol's creative process have been possible through exhibitions of his drawings and collages. In 1998, the Kunstmuseum Basel and the Andy Warhol Museum co-curated a wide-ranging exhibition of drawings beginning with juvenilia and early commercial work and ending with the late *Self-Portrait* drawings of 1985. Several recent drawing exhibitions have traced Warhol's stylistic shift from the simple elegant lines of the 1950s to the more complicated surfaces of his collages from the 1970s and 1980s. Works in these shows ranged from the whimsical and delicate hand-colored hats shown at the Paul Kasmin Gallery, New York (2006) to the more introspective, personal ballpoint pen drawings from Warhol's trip to Asia in 1956 at the Sabine Knust Gallery, Munich (2006). *Andy Warhol Public Faces, Private Lives: Collages 1975–1986* at Galerie Thaddeus Ropac, Paris presented collage portraits of famous people, from Michael Jackson to Vladimir Lenin, while the Paul Kasmin Gallery recently exhibited forty-three unique variations of the flower *Kiku*, the chrysanthemum which is the insignia of the Royal House of Japan. Finally, *Andy Warhol: Popstars* at the Albertina Museum, Vienna (2006) showcased over sixty drawings and collages of famous personalities, over half of which had never been seen before.

Whether comprehensive or selective, thematically based or medium-specific, the exhibitions undertaken in collaboration with The Warhol Foundation share the goal of making the complex oeuvre of Andy Warhol more widely known, studied and appreciated. The foundation will continue to support exhibitions that educate and enlighten the public and that expand the growing body of scholarship on Warhol's artistic practice and his place in contemporary art history.

By your kindness, caring and generosity, you are helping to remove some of that dust by aiding in my recovery and enabling me to start again creating art."—*K. Broussard, Biloxi MS*

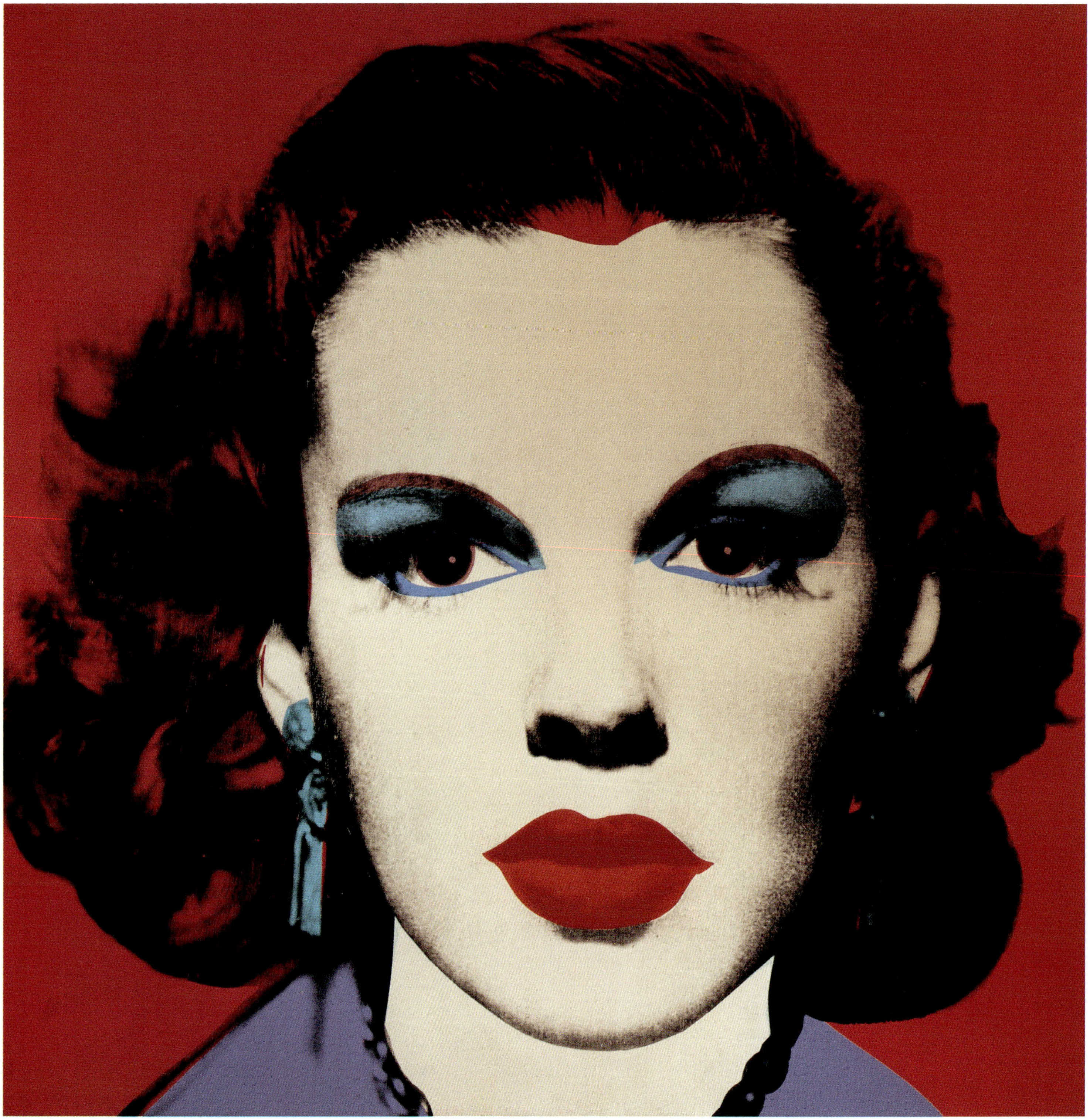

Judy Garland, c.1979, Synthetic polymer paint and silkscreen ink on canvas, 40 x 40 inches

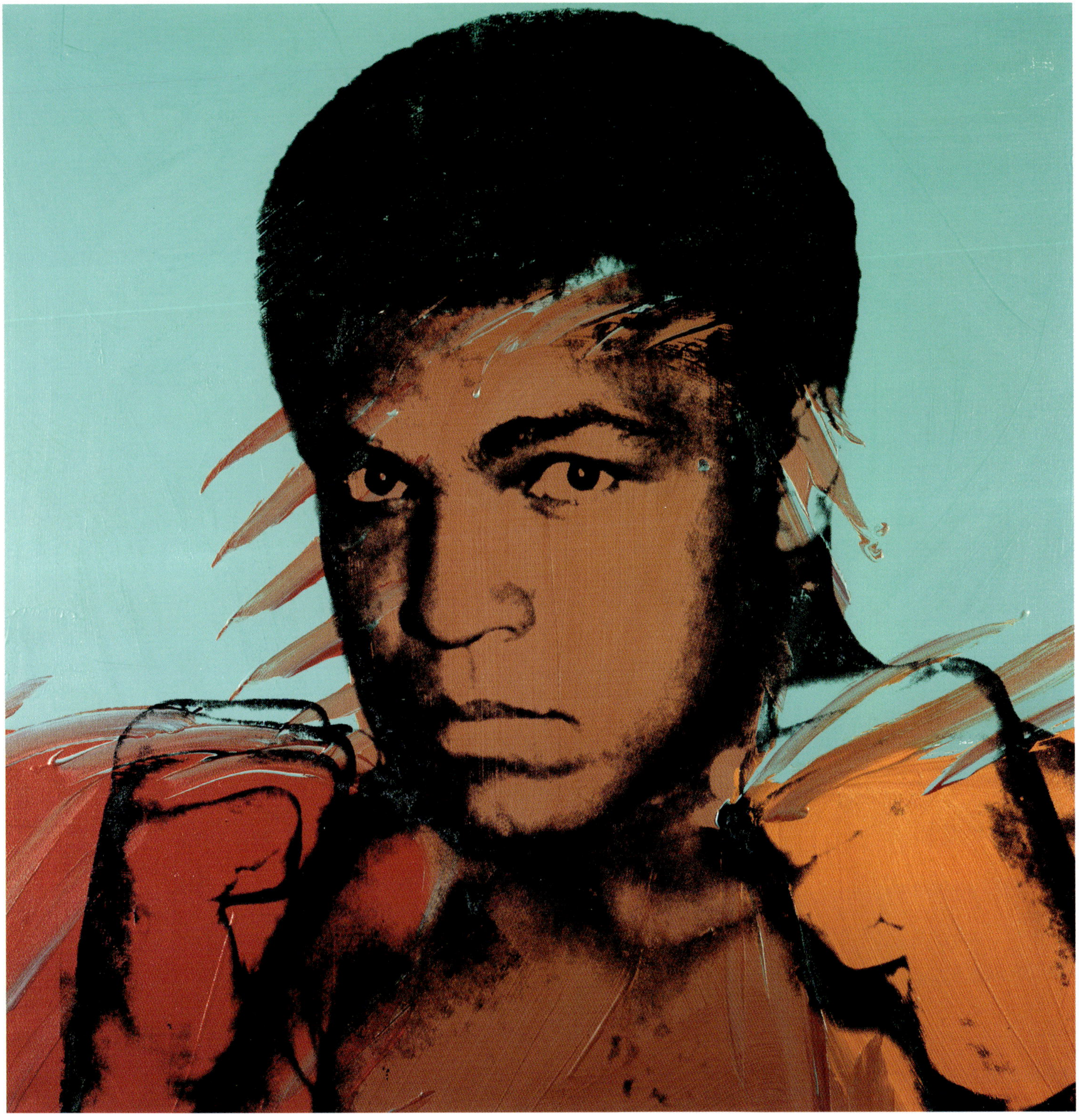

Muhammad Ali, 1977, Silkscreen ink on synthetic polymer paint on canvas, 40 x 40 inches

“Don’t pay any attention to what they write about you.

Just measure it in inches."

Catalogues Raisonné

In addition to its extensive involvement with exhibitions of Warhol's work around the world, the foundation has another significant avenue through which it supports scholarly research on Warhol: the catalogues raisonné. Work is ongoing on comprehensive, illustrated catalogues raisonné for Warhol's paintings, sculptures and drawings; his prints; and his films. Begun even before his death, these catalogues are massive undertakings, crucial to understanding the scope and depth of Warhol's artistic project and essential to the work of future generations of artists and scholars. The foundation is proud to support the research necessary for the most accurate, up to date and accessible account of its benefactor's entire artistic output.

Paintings Sculptures and Drawings

The project to assemble a comprehensive catalogue of all of Andy Warhol's paintings, sculptures, and drawings — a catalogue raisonné — was initiated by the Swiss art dealer Thomas Ammann, with Warhol's approval, in 1976. When Thomas Ammann began the project, Warhol was not yet 50 years old. Not only was he in the middle of his career, he was producing some of his most brilliant and powerful paintings at this time, such as the *Skulls* and *Hammer and Sickle* series.

In 1993, six years after Warhol's death and shortly before Thomas Ammann died, the Warhol Foundation joined Thomas Ammann Fine Art in sponsoring the catalogue raisonné. The foundation hired Neil Printz to serve as co-editor with Georg Frei of Thomas Ammann Fine Art. Kynaston McShine and Robert Rosenblum served as editorial advisors. The goal was to produce the first volume of the catalogue raisonné, which would document Warhol's painting and sculpture from the 1960s. The sheer quantity of work made by Warhol during this decade, however, required two volumes that filled three books and recorded over 2,100 works of art. Phaidon Press published *Volume 1: Paintings and Sculpture 1961–1963* in 2002. All of the 546 works in this volume were made during a rather brief but remarkably inventive period of less than three years, prior to the silver Factory at 231 East 47th Street. In 2004, Phaidon published *Volume 2: Paintings and Sculptures 1964–1969* as a set of two books, documenting over 1,500 paintings and sculptures.

The foundation is committed to funding work on the catalogue raisonné until its completion, maintaining the rigorous scholarly

"I had recently graduated from Atlanta College of Art when I was offered the opportunity to exhibit my work at the Small Gallery at Eyedrum. At the time I didn't have a lot of income, standards established by the first two volumes. In the fall of 2004, an editorial team was assembled in New York, with Neil Printz as Editor and Sally-King-Nero as Executive Editor, and research is now in progress, sponsored by the foundation. Warhol produced significantly more work during each of the decades that followed than during the 1960s. It will require four volumes to document the approximately 2,900 paintings and sculptures of the 1970s, and another four volumes to document the 1980s. It is anticipated that research and the manuscript for the next volume, *Volume 3: Paintings and Sculptures 1970–1974*, will be completed in 2008, and that subsequent volumes will be completed at two-year intervals.

Warhol's studio at 33 Union Square West — the second Factory — establishes the chronological framework for Volume 3, much as the first Factory at East 47th Street did for Volume 2. Although Warhol moved his studio to 33 Union Square West in early 1968, most of his activity was dedicated to film production and the publication of *Interview* magazine. Only a handful of portrait commissions, experimental sculptures and projects date from the period 1968–1971. This changed dramatically in 1972, when Warhol began a series of works based on the official portrait of Mao Tse-tung in Tiananmen Square, widely reproduced in popular editions of the *Quotations from Chairman Mao Tse-tung*. At this time, Warhol began to paint again with renewed vigor and concentration. Between 1970 and September 1974, when he moved his studio across Union Square to 860 Broadway, Warhol produced almost 200 paintings of Mao in a variety of sizes, ranging from 14-1/2 by 11-1/2 feet to 12 by 10 inches. During this same period he executed approximately 75 portrait commissions and 500 portrait canvases.

Warhol's portrait practice between 1970 and 1987 is documented by an extraordinary body of color polaroid photographs. It is the armature that ties his late work together, parallel to the works in series that he created with stunning regularity after 1972. During the 1970s after *Mao*, Warhol produced the following major series while working on portrait commissions: *Ladies and Gentlemen* (1975); *Russell Means (The American Indian Series)* and *Cats and Dogs* (1976); *Skulls* and *Hammer and Sickle* paintings (1976–77); *Torso* paintings (1977); *Shadows* and *Oxidations* (1978); the *Diamond Dust* paintings and the *Retrospective and Reversal* series (1978–80). Warhol's portraits and works in series operate in tandem like two strands of a double helix that make up the genetic code, in effect, of the late work. Their alternation, chapter by chapter, establishes a basic architecture for Volume 3 and the volumes to follow.

Since the catalogue raisonné is a compilation of the complete corpus of Warhol's paintings, sculptures and drawings, every work to be included must be thoroughly researched and documented. Once a work is located, it is examined by the editors first-hand. Characteristics such as color, facture, materials, dimensions and inscriptions, as well as other markings and labels are recorded at this time. In addition to its physical description and a color reproduction, the catalogue entry for each work includes its provenance, exhibition history, and citations from the scholarly literature. Entries are accompanied by supplementary illustrations and annotations; series and related groups of works are linked by introductory texts.

Warhol himself left a record of his activity that is unprecedented in its richness and detail — literally hundreds of boxes of documents, photographs and ephemera, including approximately 600 that he specifically designated as "Time Capsules". Access to the Warhol archives and materials from other public and private archives has enabled the editors to document commissions and series, to reconstruct Warhol's major exhibitions, and to place his works in chronological sequences. The catalogue raisonné is the first systematic study of Warhol's sources, techniques and development, and the most exhaustive to date. More than a list of works, each volume of the catalogue raisonné is intended to function contextually, as a chronicle of the studio.

Prints

With enthusiastic encouragement and assistance from Warhol and with information provided by Rupert Jasen Smith, Warhol's principal printer from 1977 through 1987, Frayda Feldman and Jörg Schellmann edited the first edition of *Andy Warhol Prints: A Catalogue Raisonné* in 1985, which documented 114 published edition prints and print portfolios executed from 1962 to 1985. Frayda Feldman, Co-Director of Ronald Feldman Fine Arts, New York and Jörg Schellmann, Director of Edition Schellmann, Cologne and New York had developed close working relationships with Warhol as publishers of many print projects with him in the 1980s.

and the little money I did have didn't last long. So when it came down to the installation of my drawing I began to worry. It was a relief when I was informed that I would receive a

There had been other previous efforts to document Warhol's prints: Rainer Crone's catalogue *Andy Warhol* (1970), which focused on the paintings, and Hermann Wünsche's catalogue raisonné, *Andy Warhol Das Graphische Werk 1962–1980* (1980). However, Feldman and Schellmann's catalogue raisonné, in addition to documenting Warhol's published print editions, also recorded Warhol's numerous edition trial proofs (prints pulled during the proofing process that reflect color and/or compositional changes) which more thoroughly explained Warhol's printmaking process. An introduction by Warhol's long-time supporter, Henry Geldzahler, and an essay tracing the development of Warhol's prints by the art historian Roberta Bernstein are included in the catalogue. The second edition, published by Feldman and Schellmann in 1989, included forty-eight new print editions, updated original texts, and an interview with Rupert Jasen Smith.

In 1997, ten years after Warhol's death, Frayda Feldman and Claudia Defendi, Chief Curator and Curator of Prints at the foundation, collaborated to document the artist's complete oeuvre in this medium. This revised and expanded third edition, *Andy Warhol Prints: A Catalogue Raisonné 1962–1987*, while incorporating the catalogue entries of the second edition, was entirely reorganized and presented several major changes. The most significant change was the addition of two sections, Early Printmaking and Unpublished Prints, which illustrate the extensive range of Warhol's creativity and experimentation. Early Printmaking documents works from 1962 through 1968, which were primarily hand-printed by Warhol and were not intended to be published as uniform limited editions. Unpublished Prints documents works which were predominantly created by Warhol in the 1970s and 1980s for personal and unrealized projects, or for use in magazines and advertisements. Donna de Salvo, art historian and Chief Curator and Associate Director of Programs at the Whitney Museum of American Art, contributed a text that presents an overview of Warhol's printmaking activity, while the inclusion of the text by philosopher and art critic Arthur C. Danto explores Warhol's work within a modern political and historical context.

In 2003, Feldman and Defendi published a fourth edition of the catalogue raisonné, which maintained the core of the third edition but also included a section on portraits as well as a supplement entitled Illustrated Books and Portfolios from the 1950s. This catalogue, now the authoritative reference source on the subject, illustrates the breadth of Warhol's work in printmaking and the depth of his innovations in the field, which together secure his position as one of the most important graphic artists of the twentieth century.

Film

Between 1963 and 1968 Andy Warhol directed hundreds of films, including such classics of independent American cinema as the over-five-hour *Sleep*, the eight-hour *Empire*, *The Chelsea Girls*, *Kiss*, *Blow Job*, *My Hustler*, and *Lonesome Cowboys*. In his film work he experimented with the use of real time and explored the cinematic beauty of errant moving images. He developed an underground cast of stars, many of whom appear in his Screen Tests. Beginning in 1968, Warhol collaborated with director Paul Morrissey to produce feature films such as *Flesh*, *Trash*, *Heat*, *Women in Revolt*, *Flesh for Frankenstein*, and *Blood for Dracula*.

Warhol also produced video tapes and television programs. As early as 1965, and from 1971 to 1978, he and associates Michael Netter and Vincent Fremont recorded more than a hundred hours of videotape, documenting activities in and around the Factory. The tapes, loosely referred to as the "Factory Diaries", offer rare insight into Warhol's world and work methods. By 1979 Warhol and Fremont were producing cable television programs as well as fashion and music videos, all of which were directed by Don Munroe. Warhol was executive producer — and sometimes host — of the television series *Fashion* (1979–80), *Andy Warhol's T.V.* (two series: 1980–82, 1983), and *Andy Warhol's Fifteen Minutes* (1985–87).

After Warhol's death, thousands of reels of film were found in his home, in labs, and in the Factory. These were combined with the films that Warhol himself had put on deposit at the Museum of Modern Art in 1984, and as a result of a series of grants from the Warhol Foundation, they are being preserved and documented through The Andy Warhol Film Project, a joint undertaking of MoMA and the Whitney Museum of American Art. To initiate work on a catalogue raisonné of the films, the Whitney hired film historian Callie Angell as Adjunct Curator of the Andy Warhol Film Project in 1991. After more than fifteen years of exhaustive research, Angell's *Andy Warhol Screen Tests: The*

small sum from the Warhol Foundation exhibition grant to Eyedrum to cover costs. I was able to afford necessities such as light bulbs and vinyl with some money left over for me to

Films of Andy Warhol Catalogue Raisonné was published in 2006 by Harry Abrams and the Whitney Museum of American Art.

Volume 1 of what will be a two-volume set presents a literal A to Z of Warhol's Screen Tests, three-minute, closely cropped, silent, black-and-white portraits of his friends, colleagues and acquaintances. Between 1964 and 1966 Warhol shot nearly five hundred of these portraits, capturing musicians, actors, dancers, poets, painters, art critics, curators, fashion models, socialites, celebrities and complete unknowns as they filtered through the Factory. The book — a resource of unprecedented scope and depth — presents stills from each of the 472 Screen Tests accompanied by detailed information about the film stock, its physical condition, any preservation undergone, a narrative description of "what happens" over the course of the shot and biographic information about the sitters.

Angell describes the multi-faceted value of this body of Warhol's work in the book's introduction: "These films must now be seen through added layers of cultural and art historical significance — as one of Warhol's earliest and most ambitious investigations into the art of portraiture, as his largest and most complex film series and a major achievement of his minimalist cinema, and as a detailed record of a specific period in the history of avant-garde art, a complex group portrait of an intricately interrelated art world of multiple disciplines and enormous creativity. Nevertheless, like all the Warhol films, the Screen Tests are best appreciated as living remnants not only of the mid-1960s Warhol Factory and its occupants but also of Warhol's mind and eye. The immediacy of these works and the access they provide to Warhol's creative process will, one hopes, lead to new and more fully informed interpretations of his work as well as greater understanding of the scope of his genius both as a filmmaker and an artist."

The second volume of *The Films of Andy Warhol Catalogue Raisonné* will cover the rest of Warhol's cinema. Arranged in chronological order, each film will be documented with a filmographic entry, a film materials entry, preservation information, one or more frame enlargements and possible other related illustrations, and will be further explicated in an essay which describes the content of the film, the circumstances of its making, its relation to other films and works by Warhol, and other relevant history. Warhol's released films will be further documented with individual exhibition histories and bibliographies. As in Volume 1, a lengthy introduction and a chapter on cataloguing and methodology will precede the film entries and a general bibliography will be included as well. The book will contain approximately 800 pages, with an estimated 1300 frame enlargements in both color and black-and-white, and 250 collateral illustrations. Publication is expected in two to three years.

splurge on fabric and paint. I am immensely grateful and honored that I was provided the opportunity to exhibit my work without debt." —*Alison Weldon, artist, Atlanta, GA*

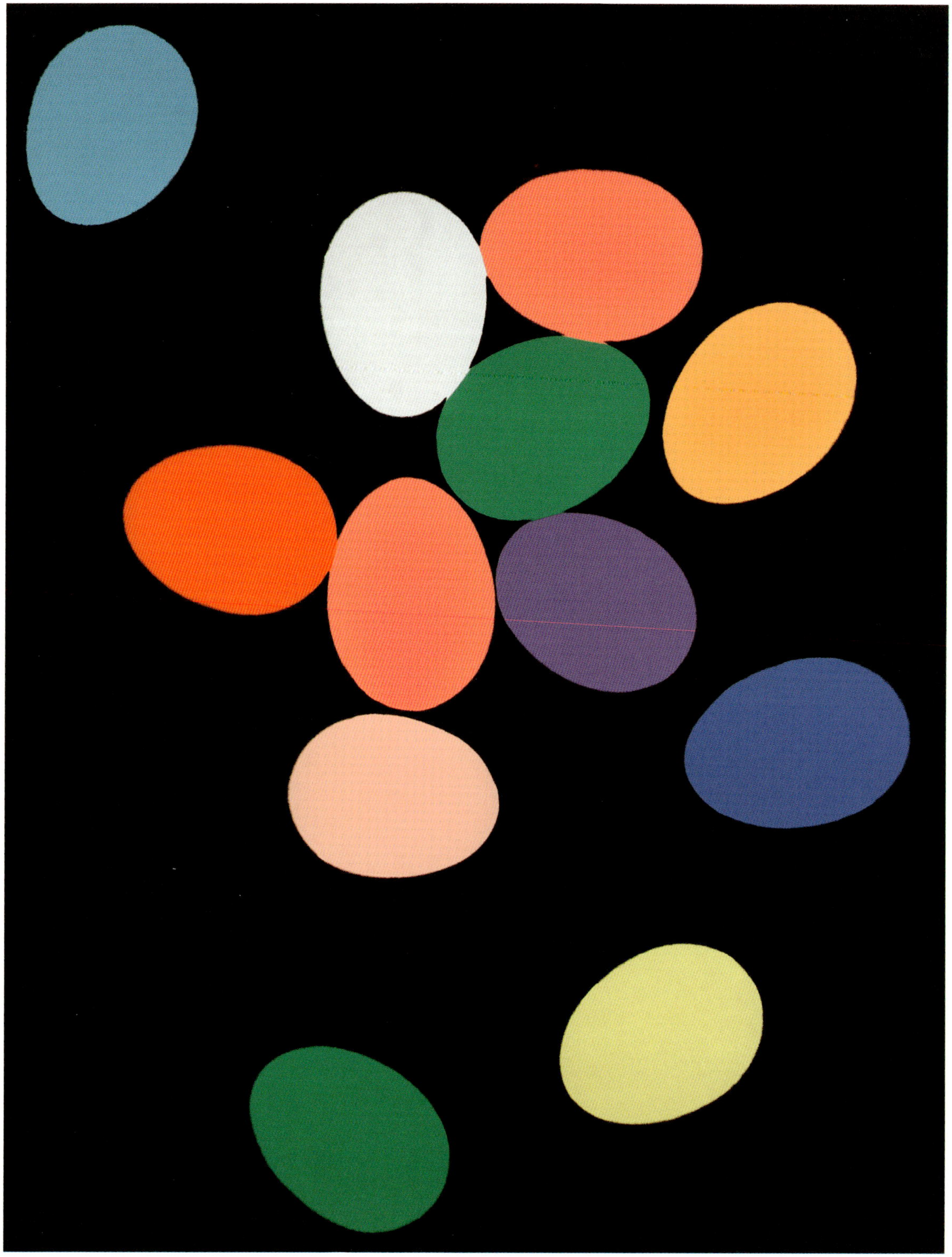

Eggs, 1982, Synthetic polymer paint and silkscreen ink on canvas, 90 x 70 inches

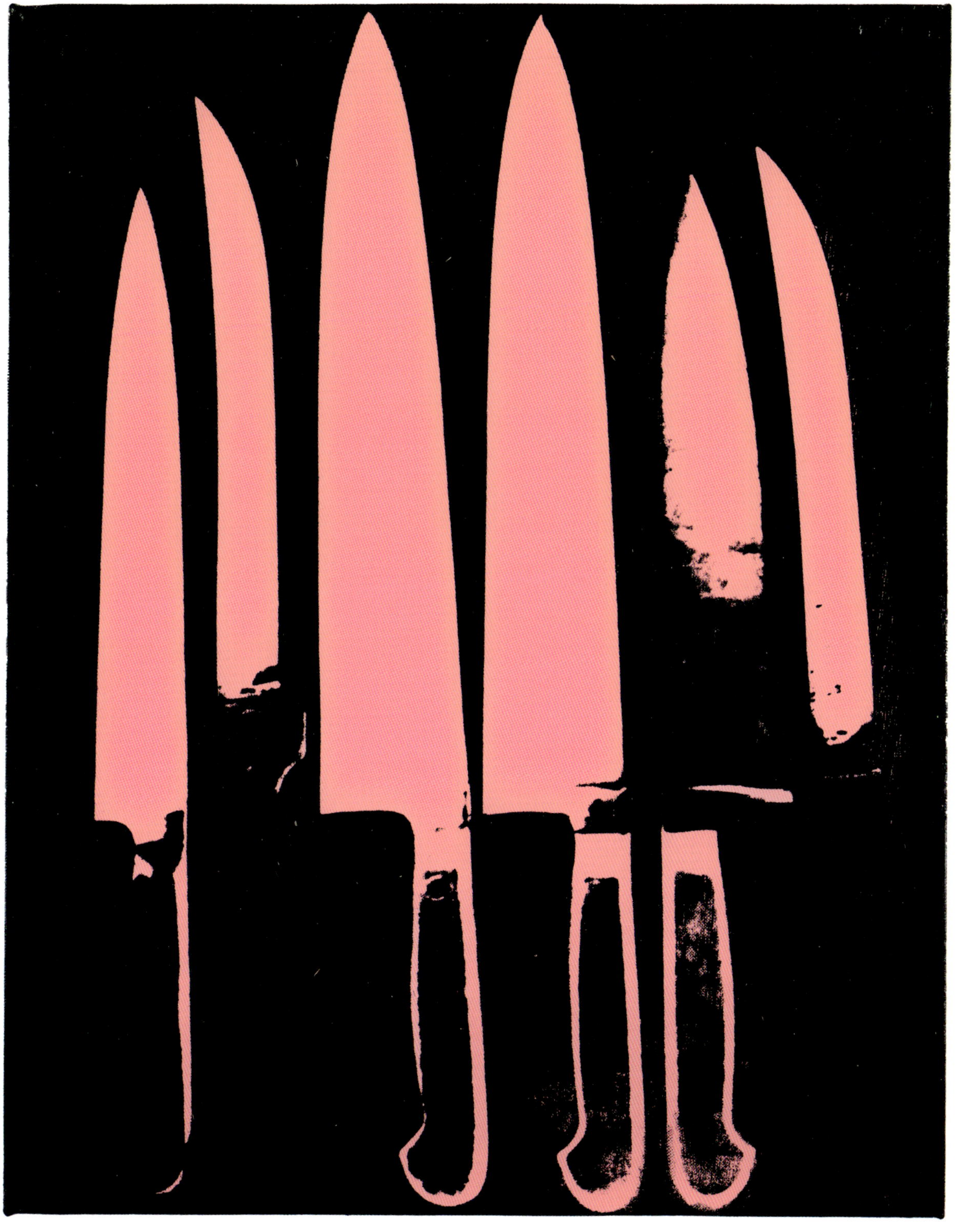

Knives, 1981, Synthetic polymer paint and silkscreen ink on canvas, 20 x 16 inches

“I don’t think less is more. More is better.

Big paintings cost more than little paintings, and magazines pay by the word.”

Museums

The foundation's work with MoMA and the Whitney Museum of American Art on the Andy Warhol Film Project is only one of several important collaborations it has undertaken with museums. The most significant and lasting relationship, of course, is with the museum it helped to found, The Andy Warhol Museum in Pittsburgh, PA. Other relationships were forged through the Museum Sales Program, which, in the 1990s, subsidized the purchase of important Warhol works by major museums around the country, including small museums otherwise unable to afford them. The recent Photographic Legacy Project has taken this generous idea one step further to make an outright gift of Warhol photographs to the nation's college and university art museums.

The Andy Warhol Museum

On September 29, 1989, the foundation signed a joint-venture agreement with the Dia Center for the Arts in New York City and the Carnegie Institute in Pittsburgh to create The Andy Warhol Museum. In 1991 the foundation made a grant of $2,000,000 to help pay for the renovation of the museum building, an eight-story, 73,000-square-foot converted warehouse on Pittsburgh's North Side, which stands only a few miles from what was Warhol's childhood home, and from Carnegie Mellon University, formerly Carnegie Institute of Technology, where he received his training in art. Designed by Richard Gluckman, with certain elements recalling Warhol's celebrated studio on East 47th Street — the first Factory — the museum opened to the public in May 1994, and to this day remains the most comprehensive single artist museum in the world.

Thomas Sokolowski was hired as Director in May 1996, and that same year the museum organized its first traveling exhibition, *Andy Warhol 1956–86: Mirror of His Time*, which traveled to Tokyo, Fukuoka and Kobe, Japan. The following year *The Warhol Look* premiered at the Whitney Museum of American Art and continued on a world tour to Toronto, London, Marseille, Sydney and Perth, Australia, ending up in Pittsburgh. In 2000 and 2001, in partnership with the Department of State's Bureau of Educational and Cultural Affairs, the museum organized *Andy Warhol : A Retrospective*, which toured 12 countries in eastern and southern Europe and included stops at the Hermitage Museum in St. Petersburg and the Pushkin Museum in Moscow. In addition to its impressive schedule of Warhol exhibitions, the museum has hosted many challenging thematic shows over the years that

"This was a very important grant for Headlands, providing crucial studio space, housing, stipends and an extraordinary community of international artists in all media to several deal with social and political issues, such as *Without Sanctuary: Lynching Photography in America*, as well as exhibitions of artists including Adrian Piper, General Idea, and Glen Ligon.

The museum's strong commitment to education is evident in the ongoing programs undertaken by its education department. In 1998, it established Artists and School Partnerships with two Pittsburgh schools, Schenley High School (Warhol's alma mater) and the High School for the Creative and Performing Arts, to teach young people about the creative process through Warhol's art and life. In 2001 and 2002, in conjunction with the *Without Sanctuary* exhibition, the museum produced the *Without Sanctuary* project which featured a diverse range of dialogues, community outreach programs and educational projects dealing with the complex issue of racism in America. Most recently, in 2006, the museum launched a major online curriculum project with its own website, *The Warhol: Resources and Lessons*.

The foundation's original gift to the museum consisted of more than 3,000 works of art, then valued at over $61,000,000. It included more than eight hundred paintings; over a thousand drawings; sculptures; numerous prints; films; and video and audio tapes. In addition to artwork, the foundation donated virtually all of Warhol's archives to the museum for its Study Center. The archival materials included scrapbooks of press clippings related to Warhol's work and his private and public life; art supplies and materials used by Warhol; posters publicizing his exhibitions and films; over 4,000 audio tapes featuring interviews and conversations between Warhol and his friends and associates; thousands of documentary photographs; an entire run of *Interview* magazine, which Warhol founded in 1969; his extensive library of books and periodicals; hundreds of decorative art objects; and many personal items.

The core of the archives, however, are its 610 Time Capsules, standard-sized cardboard boxes, which, beginning in 1974, Warhol filled with material from his everyday life, sealed and sent to storage. In 2007, the foundation made a $654,000, six-year grant to open and catalogue the contents of those capsules that still remain untouched since Warhol sealed them, and to make their photographs, newspapers, magazines, fan letters, correspondence, telephone messages, artworks, invitations, announcements and other ephemera accessible to scholars and researchers.

In 1997, the foundation donated ownership of the rights to most of Andy Warhol's film and video work to the museum. Additionally, through the Andy Warhol Film Project, the museum receives a print of each film restored by the Museum of Modern Art, as do MoMA itself and the University of California Los Angeles Film and Television Archive (which makes them available to the Los Angeles Museum of Contemporary Art as well). The museum currently has a collection of 273 preserved Warhol films and the entire Andy Warhol Video Collection of almost 4,000 videotapes. (Copies of all television material are also owned by the Museum of Television and Radio, New York and Los Angeles.) This work, crucial to understanding Warhol's work in other media, is exhibited on a regular basis in the museum's theater and galleries and is lent out for screenings and exhibitions worldwide.

Museum Sales Program

In 1992 the foundation embarked upon a project to place some of Warhol's most important pieces in museums across the country, especially those museums which did not already have significant Warhol works in their collections. The foundation enabled the museums to acquire works by selling them at a substantial discount, making each acquisition a partial gift from the foundation. Through this program, 103 major works by Andy Warhol entered the collections of 24 museums, including the Art Institute of Chicago, the Metropolitan Museum of Art, the Museum of Fine Arts, Boston, the National Portrait Gallery, the Sheldon Memorial Art Gallery at the University of Nebraska, the Walker Art Center in Minneapolis, the Whitney Museum of American Art, the Los Angeles Museum of Contemporary Art and the Baltimore Museum of Art, where they are permanently accessible to the public.

The Andy Warhol Photographic Legacy Program

The Andy Warhol Photographic Legacy Program was launched in 2007 in celebration of the foundation's 20th Anniversary. Through this unprecedented program the foundation donated over 28,500 photographs by Andy Warhol to educational institutions across the United States. More than 180 college and university museums, galleries and art collections throughout

exceptional artists from around the world. Without this generous award, Headlands would not have been able to facilitate the creation of dozens of new pieces by Carla Klein,

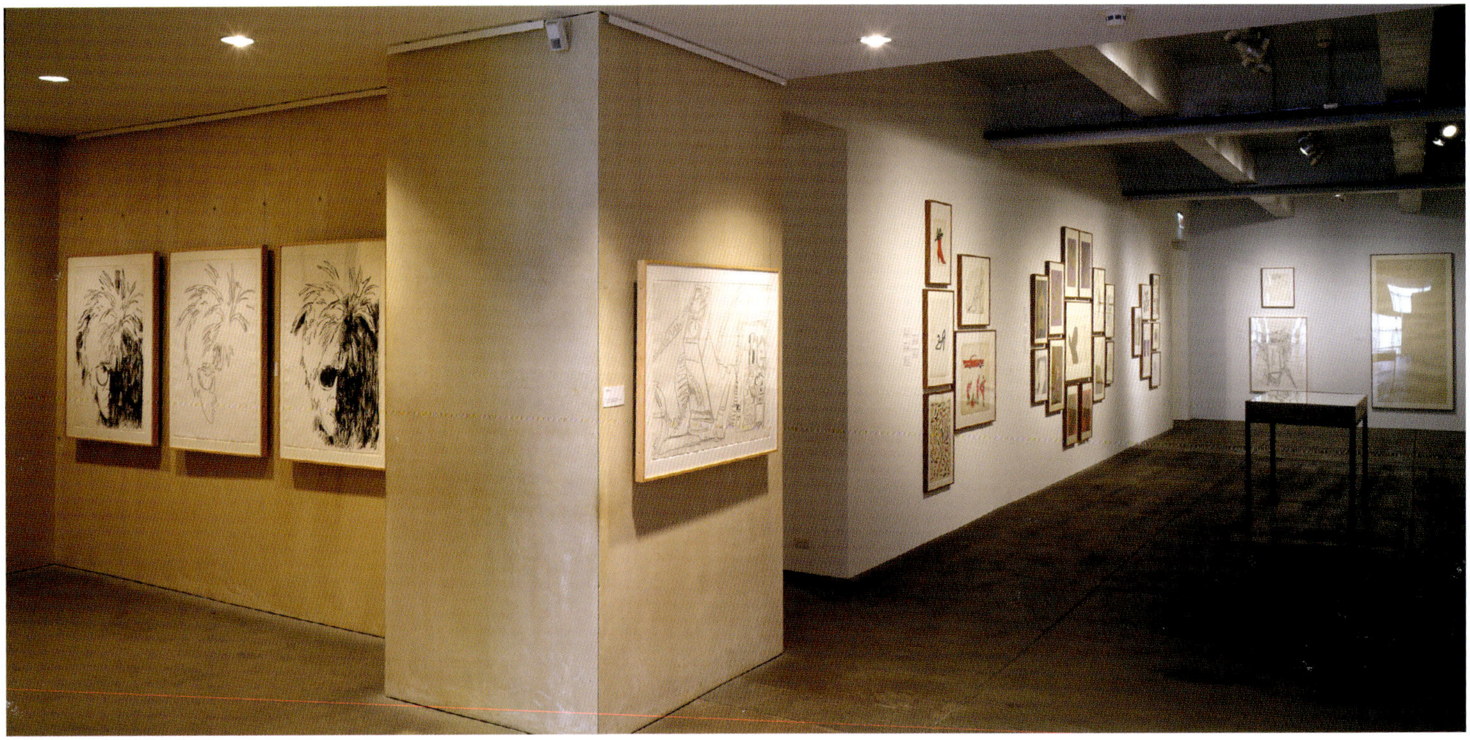

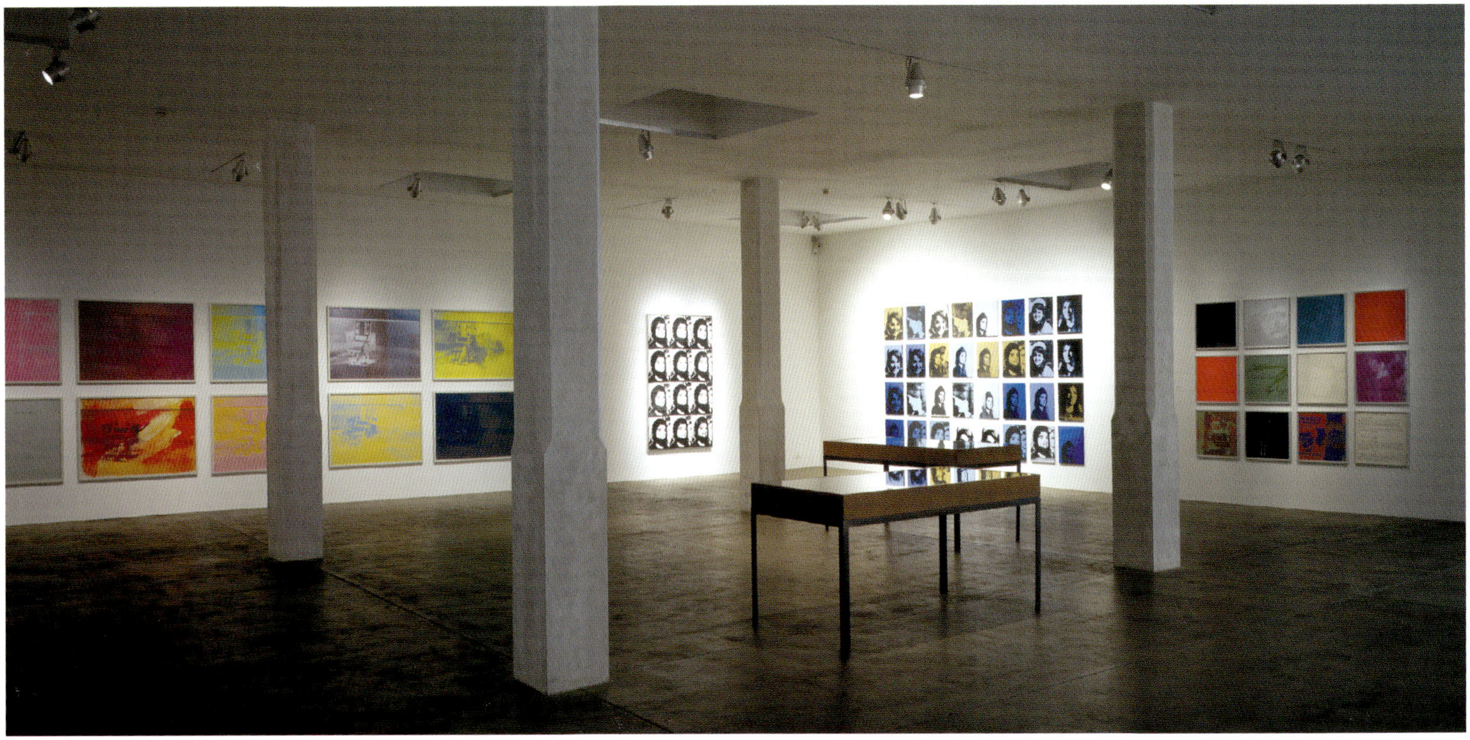

Andy Warhol Drawings, 1942–1987 **at The Andy Warhol Museum, Pittsburgh, February 27 – April 30, 2000**
Andy Warhol — Photography **at The Andy Warhol Museum, Pittsburgh, November 6, 1999 – January 30, 2000**

William Cordova, Jim Drain, Lisa Sigal, Oliver Herring and Lisa Anne Auerbach. Each of these accomplished early career artists brought a generosity of spirit and impressive work the nation participated in the program, each receiving a curated selection of original polaroid photographs and gelatin silver prints.

The portraits, celebrity snapshots, couples, nudes, painting ideas, party photos, still lifes and outdoor scenes that make up each selection demonstrate the range of Warhol's aesthetic interests and the reach of his curious and far-roaming eye. The polaroid portraits reveal the artist's profound and frank engagement with the personality in front of his camera — be it a celebrity, a beauty, a tycoon or a socialite — while the gelatin silver photographs reveal his extraordinary compositional skill, his eye for detail and his compulsive desire to document the time in which he lived.

Warhol often used these photographs as the basis for commissioned portraits, silkscreen paintings, drawings, and prints. He published three books, one posthumously, featuring his black and white photographic work: *Andy Warhol's Exposures* (1979), *America* (1985) and *Andy Warhol's Party Book* (1988). Together with the photographic exhibitions that began in the early 1990s, they offer the public a glimpse into Warhol's photographic practice.

The aim of the Photographic Legacy Program is to provide even greater access to Warhol's work and process, and to enable a wide range of individuals from communities and institutions across the country to view and study this important body of work. The participants were required only to demonstrate that they could exhibit the work and care for it properly. Through its democratic approach to distribution, the program offered institutions that did not have the means to acquire works by Warhol the opportunity to bring a significant number of photographs into their permanent collections while allowing those institutions that already had Warhol in their collections to enrich the breadth and depth of their holdings.

Through the gift of this material to teaching institutions around the country, the foundation hopes to spark interest, discussion and future scholarship about the essential role photography played in Warhol's artistic production and to draw attention to the lifelong commitment he had to the medium.

Andy Warhol Nature Preserve

In 1992 the foundation transferred the title to fifteen acres of prime ocean-front property once owned by Andy Warhol in Montauk, Long Island to the Nature Conservancy. The purpose of the donation was to preserve a section of the ecologically significant Montauk Moorlands and to promote the visual arts. As a condition of the gift, while maintaining the aesthetic and ecological attributes of the Andy Warhol Nature Preserve, the Conservancy has established an interpretive nature trail for visitors through this tract of mixed wetlands, woodlands, and coastal bluffs. The Conservancy also sponsors four or more visual arts programs at the Preserve each year including a week-long artist's residency, a photography workshop and painting classes for children and adults. Foundation support is provided on an ongoing basis to help offset program costs.

ethic to their time, and even while they reflected on their work, engaged other artists and new collaborations." —*Headlands Center for the Arts, Sausalito, CA*

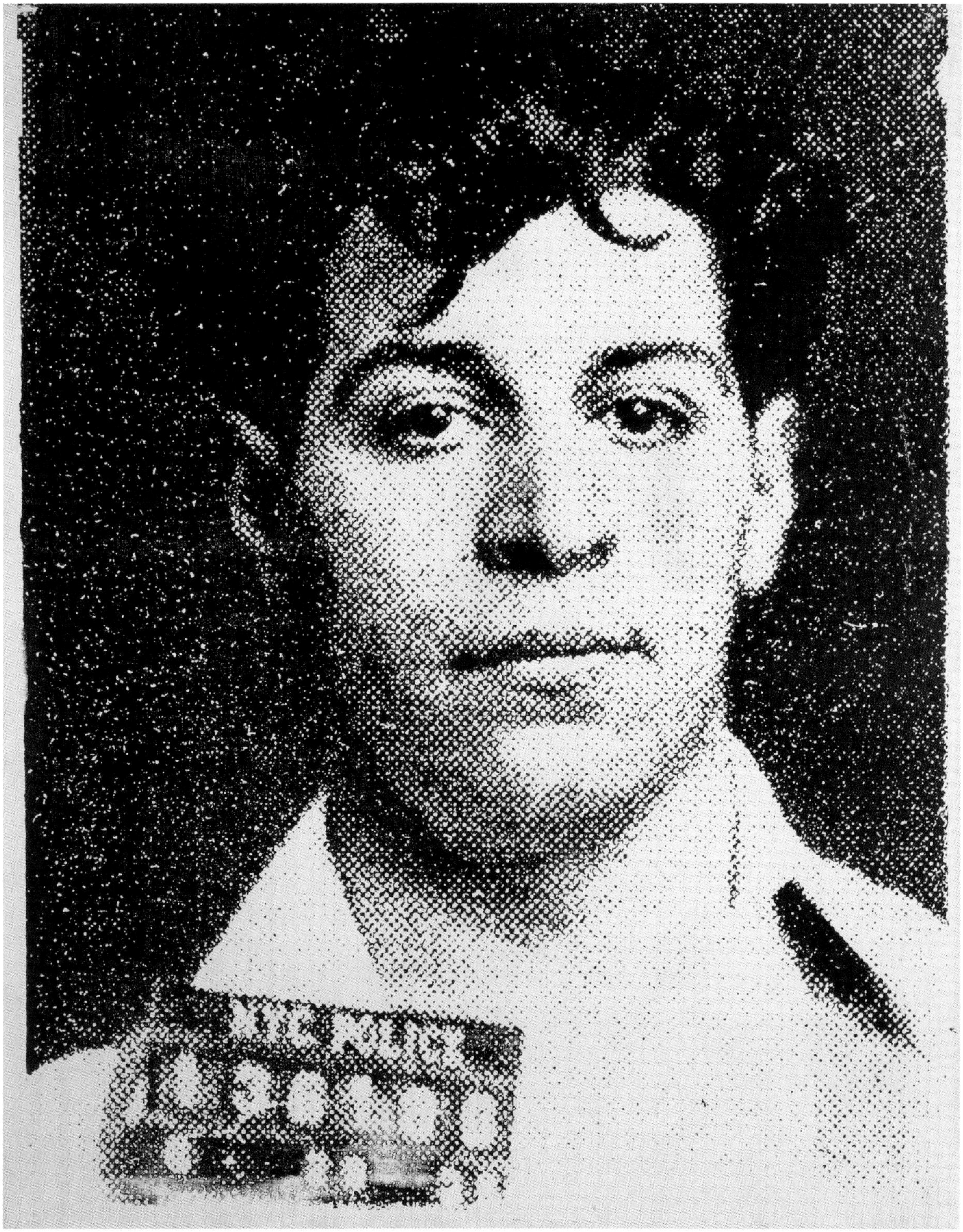

Most Wanted Men No. 12, Frank B., 1964, Silkscreen on gesso on canvas, 48 x 35 inches

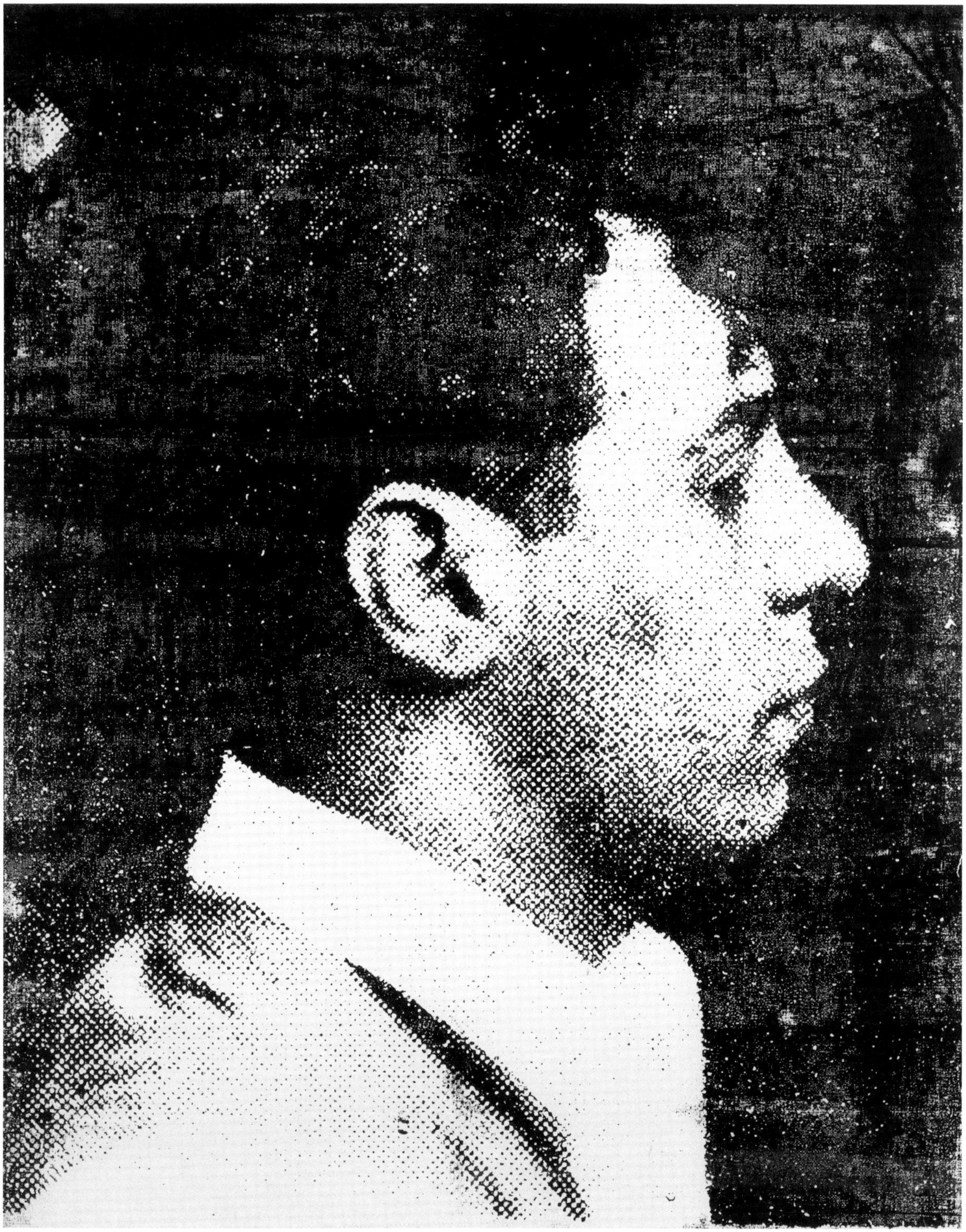

Most Wanted Men No. 12, Frank B., 1964, Silkscreen on gesso on canvas, 48 x 39 inches

“Publicity is like eating peanuts.

Once you start you can't stop."

Licensing

"I'll endorse with my name any of the following: clothing, AC-DC, cigarettes, small tapes, sound equipment, ROCK 'N ROLL RECORDS, anything, film, and film equipment, Food, Helium, Whips, MONEY!! love and kisses ANDY WARHOL."
— Village Voice Classified, 1966.

In 1987 the Warhol Foundation took ownership of the copyrights and trademarks which were in Warhol's possession at the time of his death. As representatives of one of the most influential and prolific artists of the 20th century, the foundation takes very seriously its responsibility to uphold and enhance the legacy of Andy Warhol. The foundation is committed to making Warhol's work accessible to audiences and critics around the world, and to supporting and encouraging new scholarship.

As Warhol's critical reputation has grown over the past twenty years, requests to use the foundation's copyrights and trademarks have steadily increased. The foundation has developed a two-pronged approach to licensing that distinguishes between commercial and non-commercial requests. In an effort to encourage artists and scholars to make use of its vast archive of Warhol images, the foundation charges only nominal fees to those wishing to reproduce artworks for educational and creative purposes. For more income-generating projects however, the foundation charges licensing fees commensurate with those in the commercial market.

The revenues generated through licensing fees have grown significantly over the past ten years — from just over $400,000 in 1997 to over $2,000,000 in 2007 — and are able to support more and more of the foundation's activities. Recognizing the potential for growth and creative engagement with the market, the foundation appointed its first Director of Licensing in 1998 and shortly thereafter hired an additional full time licensing staff member.

While Warhol's work speaks eloquently — and emblematically — of its time, its conceptual potency transcends eras and art movements. Warhol's artwork, public life and, most importantly, his seamless fusion of the two, continue to inspire creative thinkers worldwide. The licensing program works with licensees who understand Warhol's cultural currency and who create products that reflect his maverick approach to art making, his ability to present the familiar from unusual perspectives and his sophisticated sense of design. Warhol-branded products maintain Warhol's relevance to visual and consumer culture.

"Our involvement with the Warhol Initiative came at a truly critical time for the organization. Infrastructure and systems desperately needed shoring up. Programs needed

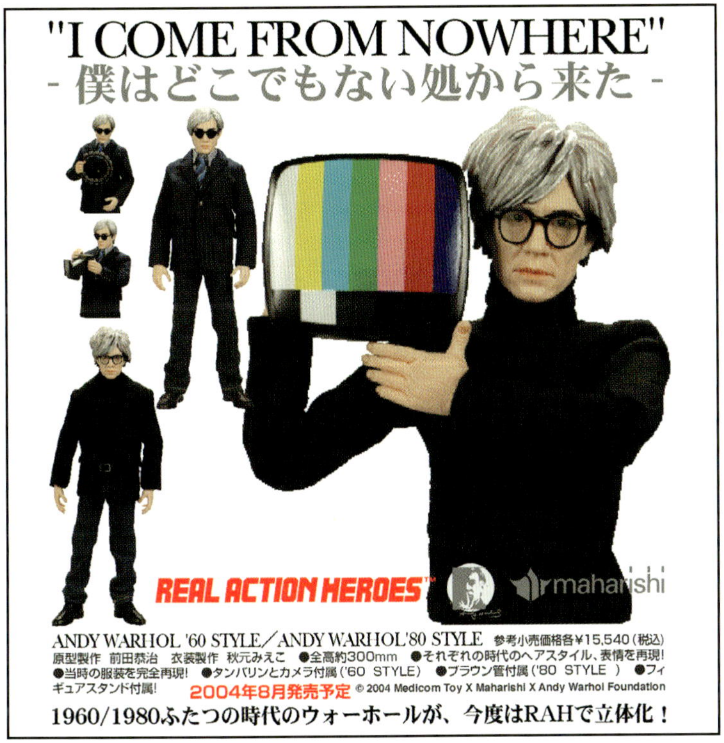

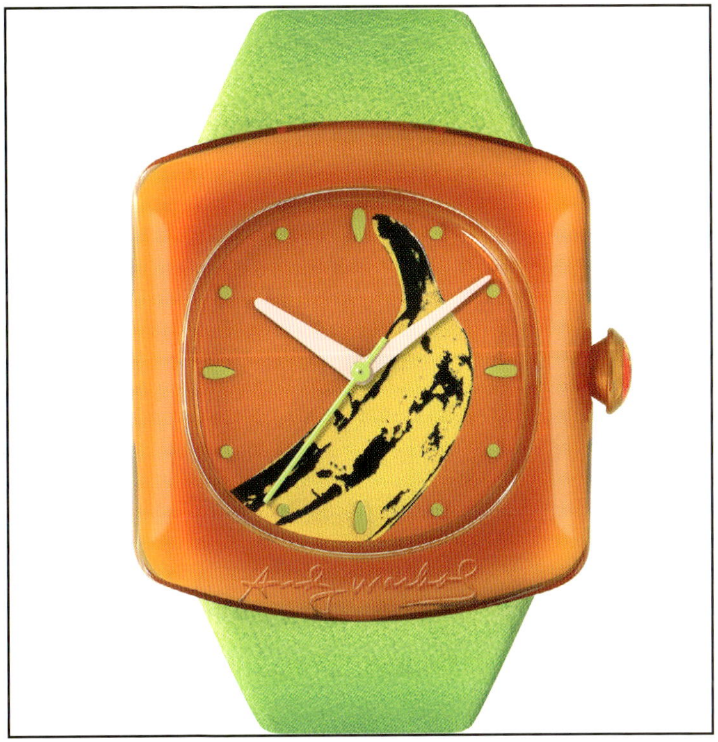

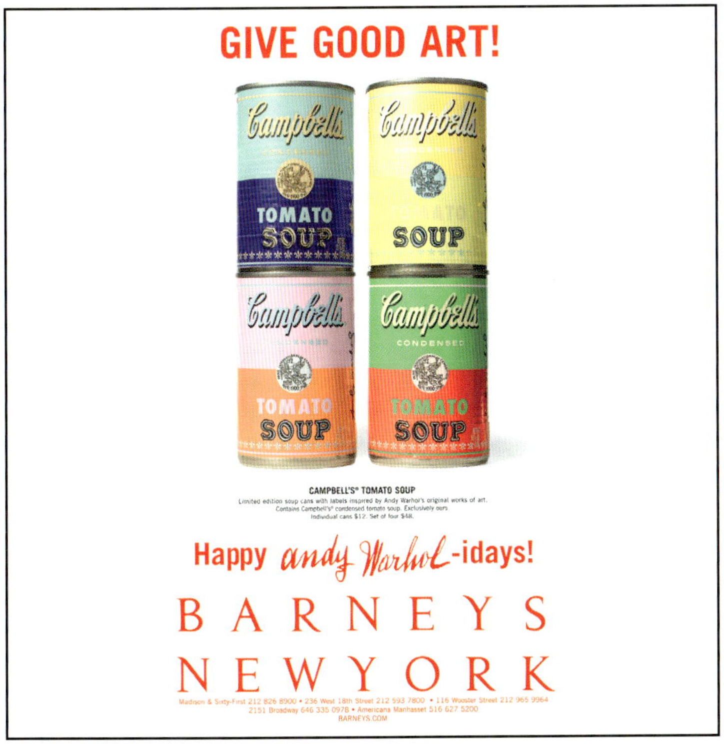

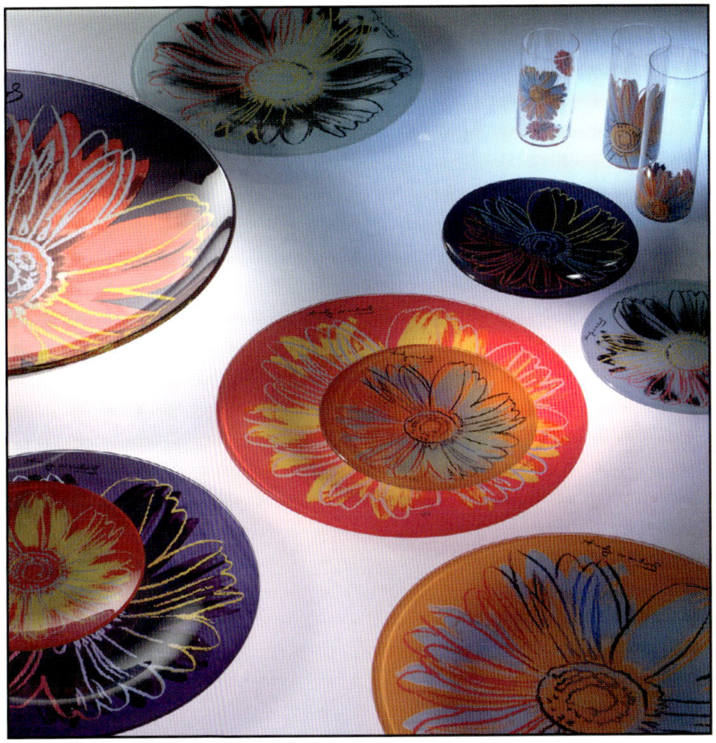

upper left: **Advertisement for Warhol Action Figure by Maharishi, 2004;** upper right: **Andy Warhol Watch by Seiko, 2006;** lower left: **Advertisement for Barneys New York *Happy Andy Warhol-idays* promotion featuring Limited Edition Andy Warhol Campbell's Soup, 2006;** lower right: **Andy Warhol Serving Plates by Rosenthal, 2003**

examination and clarification. Most importantly, the structure, priorities and future direction of the founder-run company needed to be addressed in a broad, systematic and

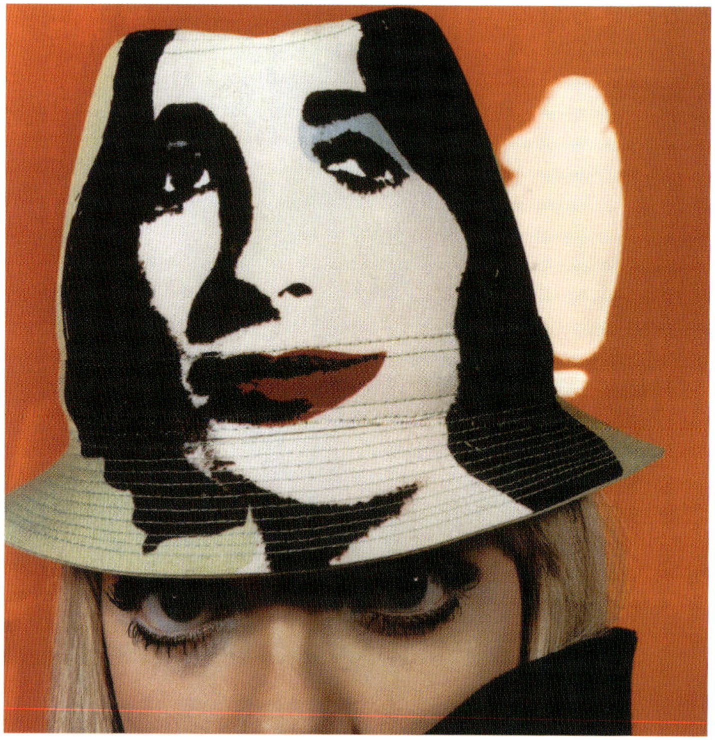

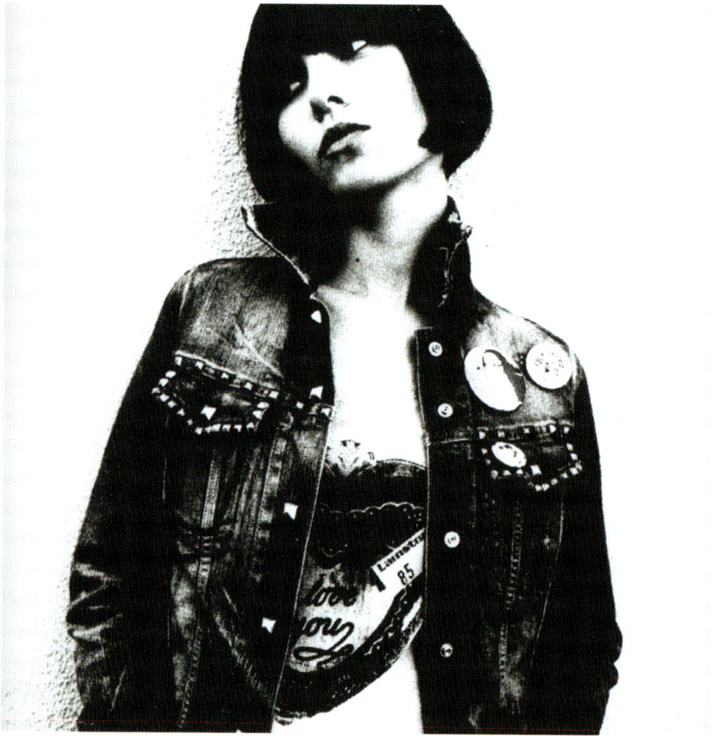

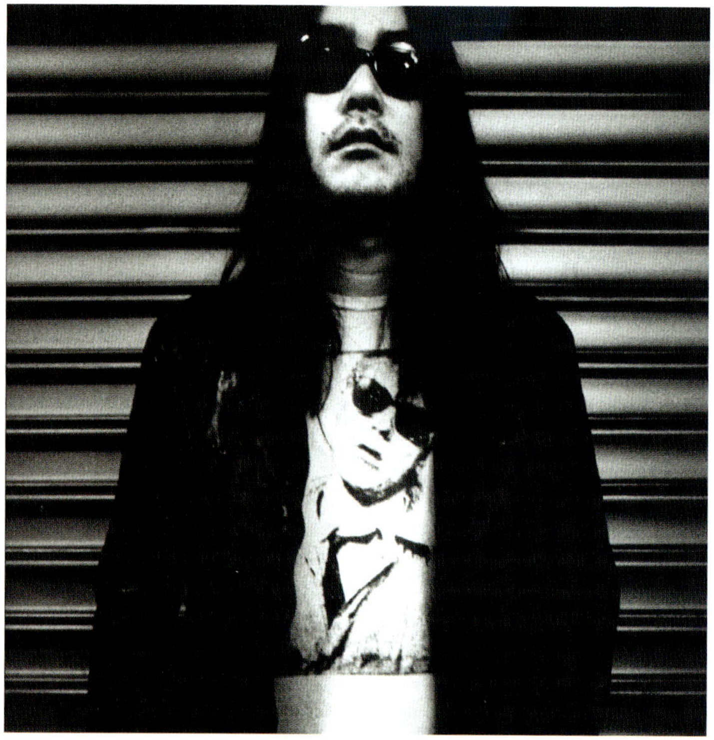

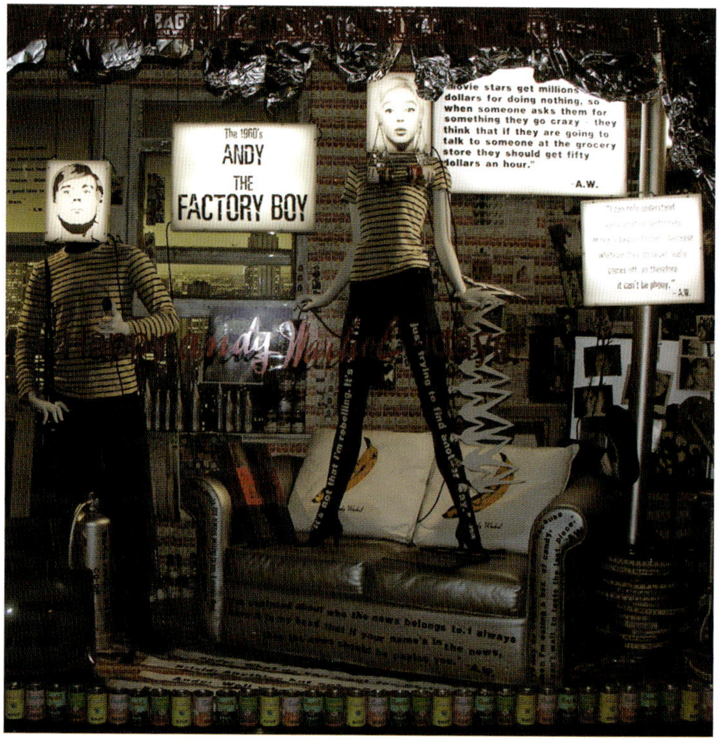

upper left: **Andy Warhol Hat by Philip Treacy, 2004;** upper right: **Andy Warhol Apparel By Hysteric Glamour, 2006, Model: Mia Tazawa (M.A.friday);** lower left: **Andy Warhol Apparel By Hysteric Glamour, 2006;** lower right: **Andy Warhol Store Window for Barneys New York *Happy Andy Warhol-idays* promotion, 2006**

clear-headed manner. While challenges remain in each of these areas, great progress has been made. It's no exaggeration at all to say that this progress would not have been

In 2001, the foundation entered into an exclusive agreement with the licensing agency The Beanstalk Group to help it identify best-in-class licensees in North America and Europe. Sanrio Far East, another licensing agency, has helped the foundation expand its licensing activities in Japan since 2003. With the hiring of a third full-time staff member in 2004 and the publication of a dynamic, visually lush guide for licensees in 2005, the foundation has been able to increase the quality and quantity of Warhol licensees worldwide, which has greatly boosted the revenue generated by the licensing program.

Some highlights of recent years include license agreements with Hysteric Glamour, Levi's, Paul Frank and Uniqlo for apparel; Burton for snowboards and apparel; Philip Treacy for hats; Rosenthal for china and glassware; S.T. Dupont for pens and lighters; Royal Elastics and Adidas for footwear; Robert Lee Morris for Jewelry; Seiko for watches; Campbell's Soup Company for soup; and Maharishi for collectibles. In 2003 Andy Warhol was honored by the United States Postal Service when it issued a commemorative postage stamp featuring Warhol's *Self-Portrait* from 1964. That same year the French Postal Service produced a stamp using one of Warhol's *Marilyn* images from 1967.

In addition to product licensing, the foundation also licenses the use of Warhol's artwork and name for various advertisements and special promotions. The recent Barneys New York holiday campaign entitled "Happy Andy Warholidays" featured Warhol images and quotes on all Barneys catalogues, window and in-store displays, and promotional materials throughout the United States. In order to ensure its access to high-profile projects of this scale, the foundation has signed a representation agreement with Corbis, an industry leader in licensing digital imagery.

The foundation has always rigorously protected itself against unauthorized uses of its copyrights and trademarks. Through outside counsel and in conjunction with Artists Rights Society, a preeminent copyright, licensing, and monitoring organization for visual artists, the foundation aggressively pursues and takes appropriate action against all unlawful uses of its intellectual property.

Looking forward, the licensing program will continue to look to Andy Warhol's life and work for inspiration and will seek out partnerships with those who understand the contemporary relevance and resonance of his practice. As Warhol himself famously said, "Being good in business is the most fascinating kind or art."

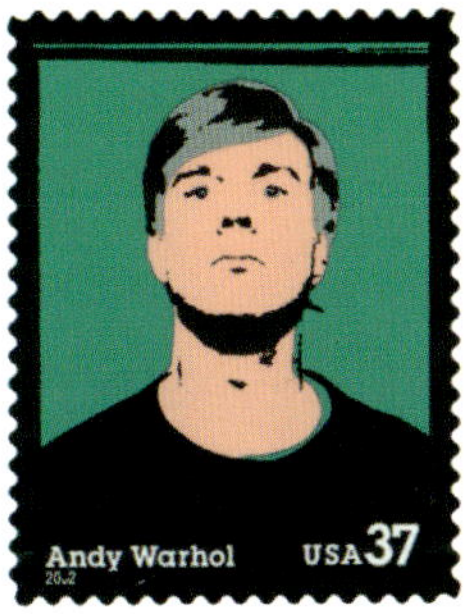

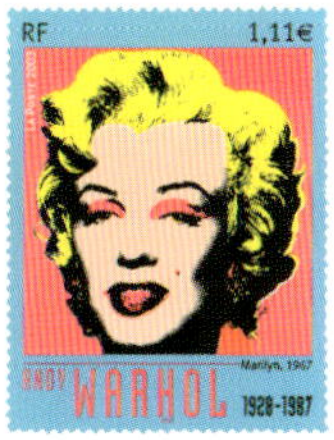

Andy Warhol United States Postage Service Stamp, 2002
Andy Warhol La Poste Stamp, 2003

possible without the Warhol Initiative." —*Legion Arts Cedar Rapids, IA*

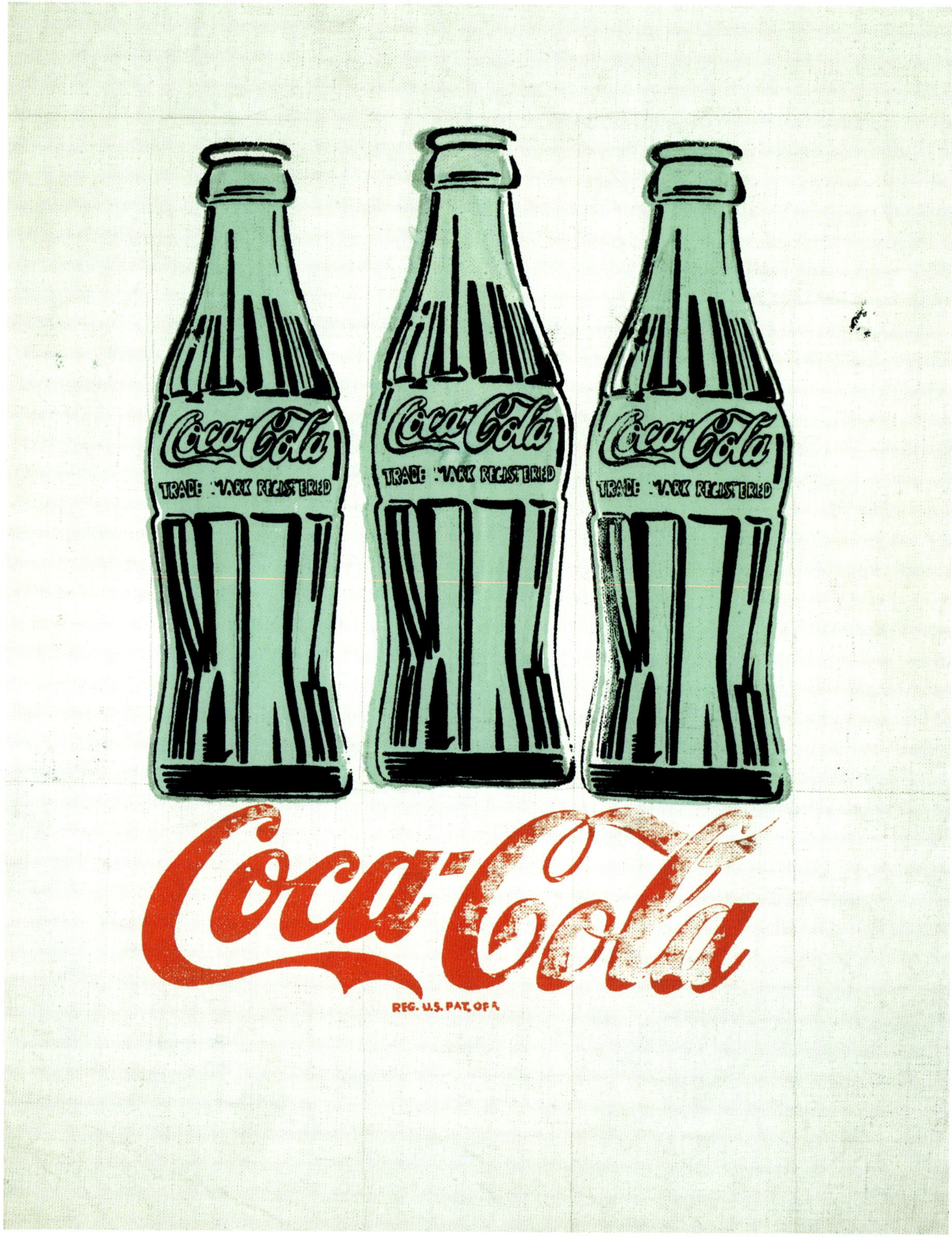

Three Coke Bottles, 1962, Synthetic polymer paint and silkscreen ink on canvas, 20 x 16 inches

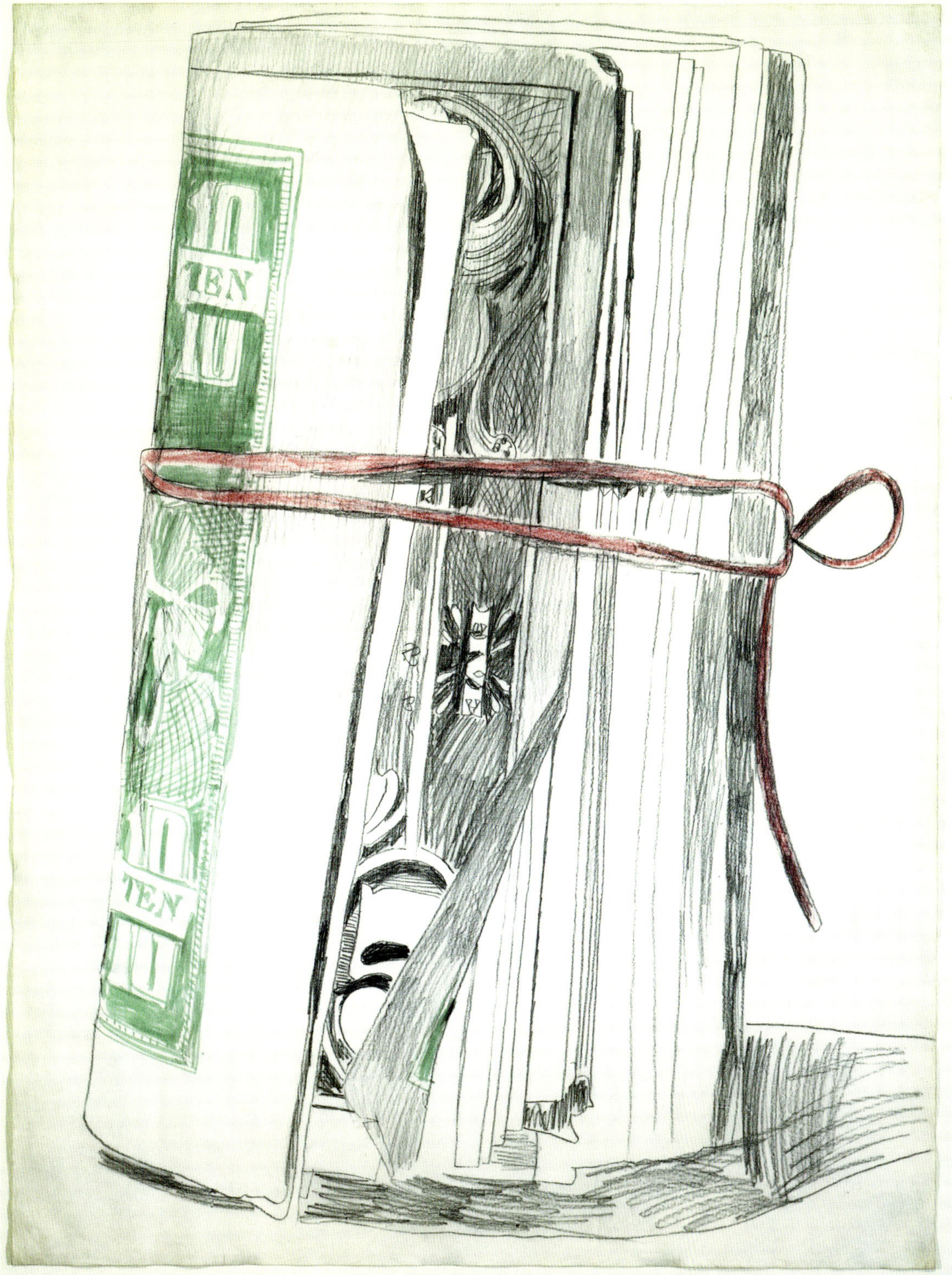

Roll of Bills, 1962, Pencil, crayon and felt-tip pen on paper, 40 x 301/8 inches

“Making money is art and working is art

and good business is the best art.”

Sales

Since its founding in 1987, the Andy Warhol Foundation has sold works of art to earn annual income and to build its cash endowment. The foundation's sales program includes themed exhibitions at galleries both in the United States and abroad, as well as sales of individual works to institutions, private collectors, and galleries. Funds raised in this way are used exclusively to support its grantmaking program.

The storage and maintenance of the remaining collection, along with the scholarship and business activity that accompany it, account for a large portion of the foundation's operating expenses. Vincent Fremont is the exclusive agent for the sale of foundation-owned Warhol paintings, sculpture, and drawings. Timothy Hunt acts as the exclusive agent for foundation-owned Warhol prints, unique prints, printed graphic material, and photography.

"I know when I say "thank you" from the bottom of my heart I am also speaking for hundreds of other artists that your foundation helped." —*S. Halat, Ocean Springs, MS*

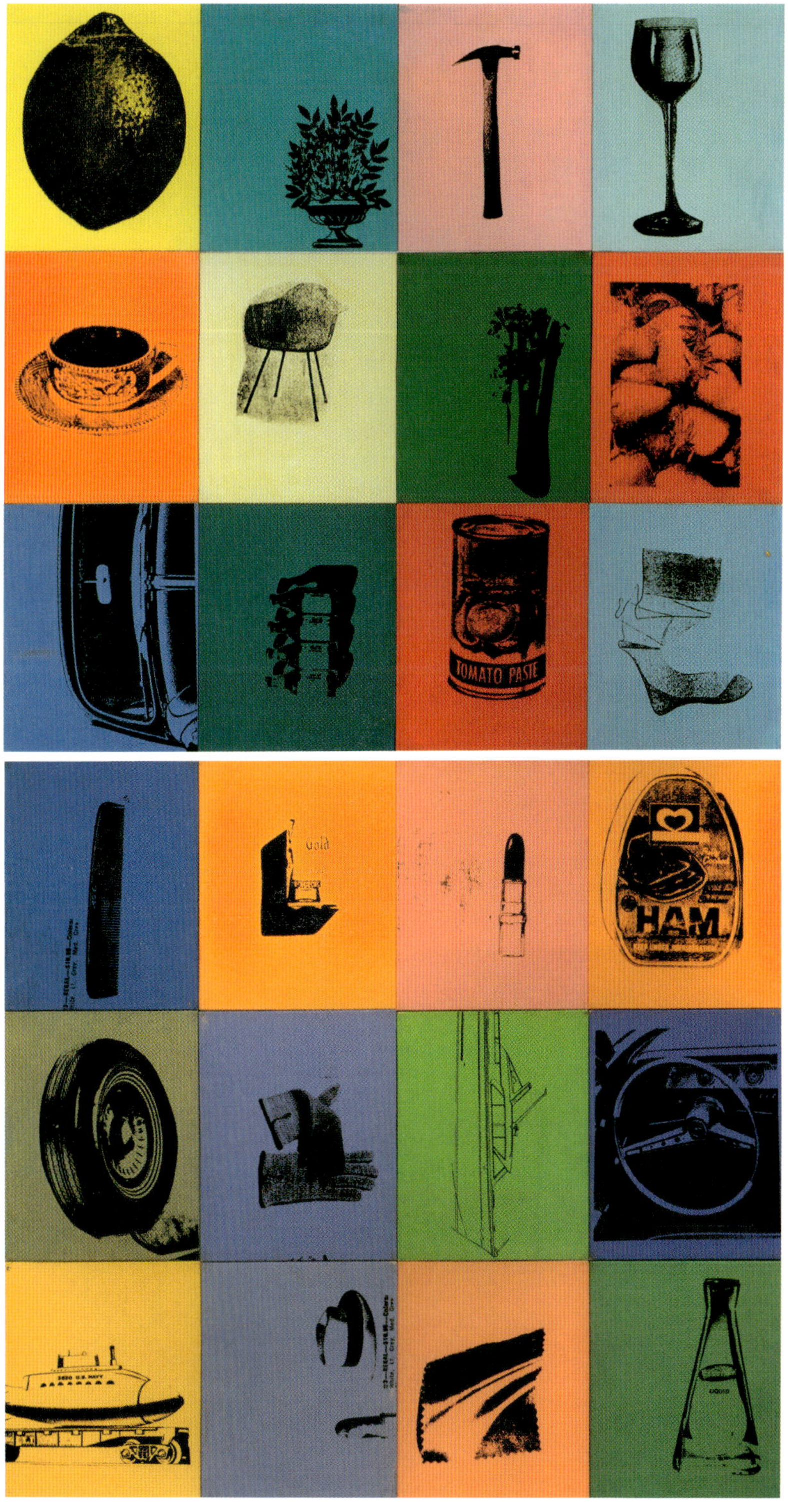

Corporate Trade Ads (Container Corporate America), 1963, Synthetic polymer paint and silkscreen ink on canvas, each panel 10 x 8 inches

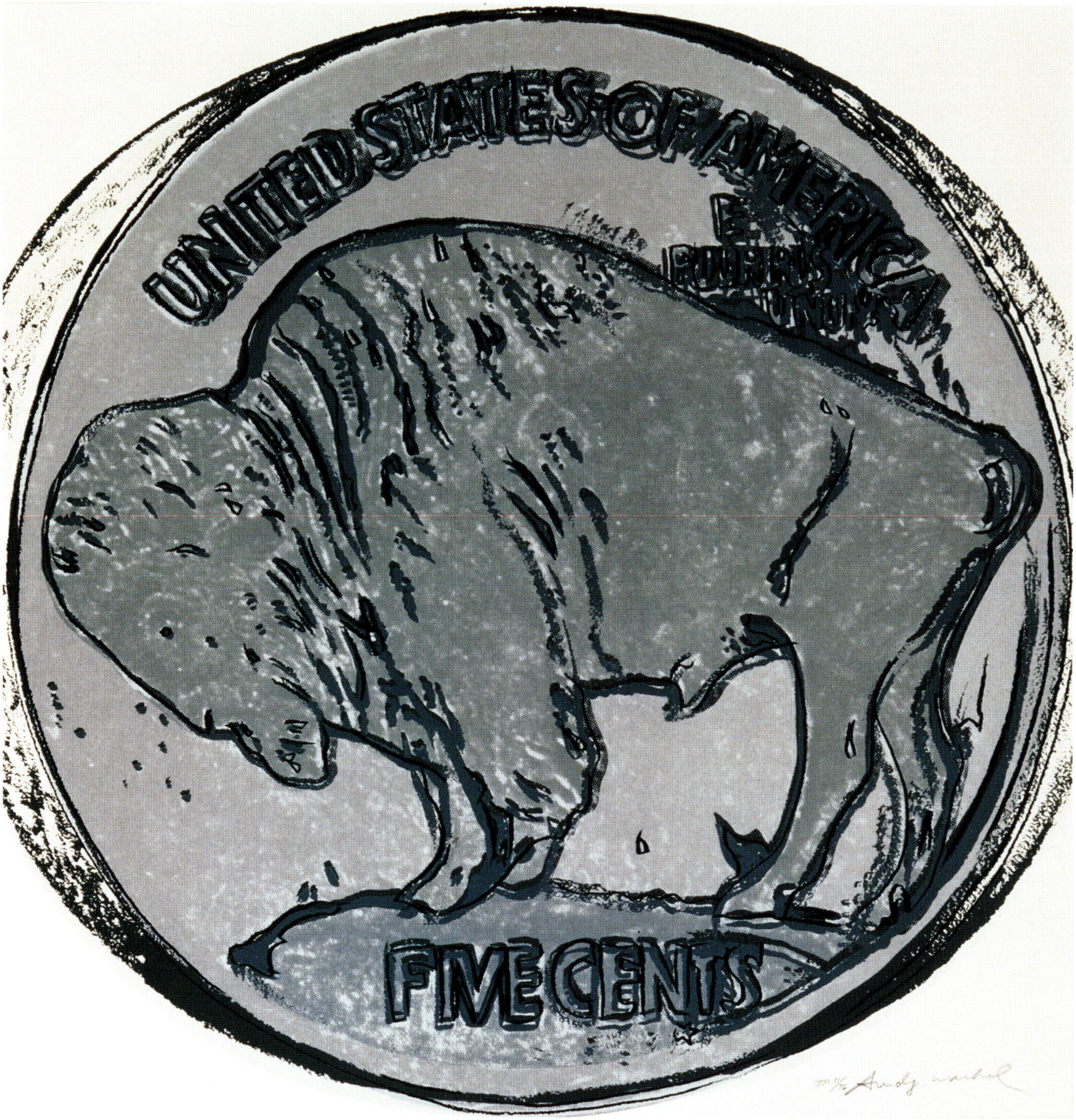

Cowboys & Indians: Buffalo Nickel, 1986, Screen-print on Lenox Museum Board, 36 x 36 inches

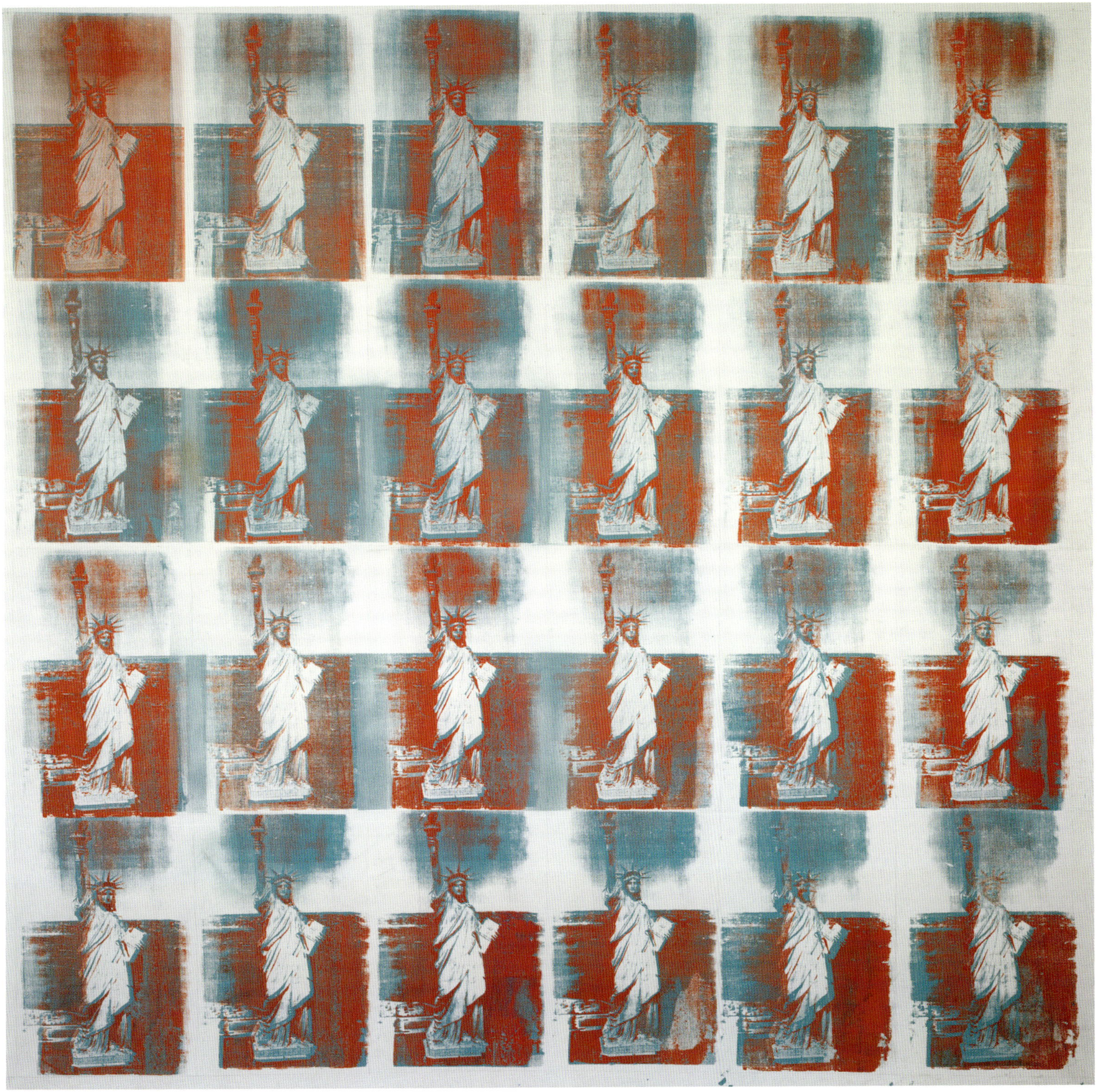

Statue of Liberty, 1963, Synthetic polymer paint and silkscreen ink on canvas, 78 x 80 2/3 inches

“Money is money. It doesn’t matter if I’ve worked hard or easy for it.

I spend
it
the same."

Financial Statements

Independent Auditors' Report

The Board of Directors
The Andy Warhol Foundation
for the Visual Arts, Inc.

We have audited the accompanying statement of financial position (modified cash basis) of The Andy Warhol Foundation for the Visual Arts, Inc. (the "Foundation") as of April 30, 2006 and April 30, 2005 and the related statements of activities (modified cash basis) and cash flows (modified cash basis) for the years then ended. These financial statements are the responsibility of the Foundation's management. Our responsibility is to express an opinion on these financial statements based on our audits.

We conducted our audits in accordance with auditing standards generally accepted in the United States of America. Those standards require that we plan and perform the audit to obtain reasonable assurance about whether the financial statements are free of material misstatement. An audit includes examining, on a test basis, evidence supporting the amounts and disclosures in the financial statements. An audit also includes assessing the accounting principles used and significant estimates made by management, as well as evaluating the overall financial statement presentation. We believe that our audits provide a reasonable basis for our opinion.

As described in note 1, the financial statements are prepared on a modified cash basis of accounting, which is a comprehensive basis of accounting other than accounting principles generally accepted in the United States of America.

In our opinion, the financial statements referred to above, present fairly, in all material respects, the financial position (modified cash basis) of The Andy Warhol Foundation for the Visual Arts, Inc. at April 30, 2006 and April 30, 2005 and its activities (modified cash basis) and its cash flows (modified cash basis) for the years then ended on the basis of accounting described in note 1.

August 10, 2006

Statement of Financial Position

(Modified Cash Basis)

	April 30, 2006	April 30, 2005
Assets		
Cash	$ 15,040,717	$ 20,705,452
Investments, at market (notes 1 and	181,408,928	143,186,458
Purchased interest	97,695	48,463
Security deposits (note 5)	66,916	66,916
Artworks (note 1)	14,912,431	16,657,362
Total assets	**$ 211,526,687**	**$ 180,664,651**
Liabilities and Net Assets		
Liabilities		
Commissions and other payables	$ 4,051,239	$ 3,697,073
Deferred revenue — deposits received on sale of artworks	18,000	100,000
Authorized but unpaid grants (notes 1 and 5)	5,868,877	4,300,451
Total liabilities	**9,938,116**	**8,097,524**
Unrestricted net assets	201,588,571	172,567,127
Total liabilities and unrestricted net assets	**$ 211,526,687**	**$ 180,664,651**

See notes to financial statements.

Statement of Activities
(Modified Cash Basis)

	Year Ended April 30, 2006	Year Ended April 30, 2005
Revenue		
Interest and dividends	$ 4,344,664	$ 3,720,446
Royalties and licensing fees	2,173,707	1,956,228
Other	47,656	17,468
Total revenue	6,566,027	5,694,142
Expenditures		
Grants authorized — net (notes 1 and 5)	9,619,280	2,438,030
Administrative and general		
Payroll and related expenses (note 4)	2,896,826	2,781,697
Directors' fees	151,667	139,167
Legal and accounting fees	312,306	379,134
Consulting fees	36,376	16,471
Curatorial and conservation expenses	397,103	288,910
Appraisal fees	4,744	4,525
Insurance	212,276	258,534
Meetings and travel	209,337	172,296
Federal excise tax (note 3)	184,000	116,000
Art storage and related expenses (note 5)	409,727	396,969
Office expenses	181,784	155,615
Licensing expenses	11,521	80,579
Rent (note 5)	223,212	176,643
Catalogue Raisonné (note 5)	18,100	18,991
Other (see page 12)	194,443	257,115
Total administrative and general	5,443,422	5,242,646
Total expenditures	15,062,702	7,680,676
(Deficiency) of revenue to cover expenditures before other additions (deductions)	(8,496,675)	(1,986,534)
Other additions (deductions)		
Net gain on sale of investments	4,192,109	2,198,574
Net unrealized gain on investments (note 1)	19,301,353	2,489,051
Investment advisory fees	(560,810)	(551,736)
Net gain on sale of artworks	16,251,949	12,646,322
Commissions on sale of artworks (note 5)	(1,664,967)	(1,393,196)
Expenses relating to the Estate of Andy Warhol (note 5)	(1,515)	(1,636)
Increase in unrestricted net assets	**29,021,444**	**13,400,845**
Unrestricted net assets, beginning of year	**172,567,127**	**159,166,282**
Unrestricted net assets, end of year	**$ 201,588,571**	**$ 172,567,127**

See notes to financial statements.

Statement of Cash Flows

(Modified Cash Basis)

	Year Ended April 30, 2006	Year Ended April 30, 2005
Cash flows from operating activities		
Increase in unrestricted net assets	$ 29,021,444	$ 13,400,845
Adjustments to reconcile increase in unrestricted net assets to net cash (used in) operating activities		
Net (gain) on sale of investments	(4,192,109)	(2,198,574)
Net unrealized (gain) on investments	(19,301,353)	(2,489,051)
Net (gain) on sale of artworks	(16,251,949)	(12,646,322)
(Increase) in purchased interest	(49,232)	(11,896)
Decrease in accounts receivable and deposits	-	4,683
Increase in commissions and other payables	354,166	108,641
Increase (decrease) in deferred revenue — deposits received on sale of artworks	(82,000)	75,000
Increase (decrease) in authorized but unpaid grants	1,568,426	(3,684,441)
Net cash (used in) operating activities	(8,932,607)	(7,441,115)
Cash flows from investing activities		
Proceeds from sale of artworks	17,996,880	14,282,597
Proceeds from sale of investments	103,871,178	104,703,078
Purchase of investments	(118,600,186)	(108,434,054)
Net cash provided by investing activities	3,267,872	10,551,621
Increase (decrease) in cash	**(5,664,735)**	**3,110,506**
Cash balance, beginning of year	**20,705,452**	**17,594,946**
Cash balance, end of year	**$ 15,040,717**	**$ 20,705,452**

See notes to financial statements.

Notes to Financial Statements
(Modified Cash Basis)
April 30, 2006

Note 1 – Summary of significant accounting policies

Operations
The Andy Warhol Foundation for the Visual Arts, Inc. (the "Foundation"), a New York not-for-profit corporation, was established in accordance with the terms of the will of Andy Warhol. The Foundation was formed for the purpose of advancing the visual arts including, without limitation, the study, creation, preservation, exhibition, public understanding and appreciation thereof.

Basis of accounting
The policy of the Foundation is to prepare its financial statements on the basis of cash receipts and disbursements modified to record investments at market, purchased interest, security deposits, commissions payable, deferred revenue and authorized but unpaid grants. Accordingly, certain revenue and the related assets are recognized when received rather than earned and certain expenses are recognized when paid rather than when the obligation is incurred.

Investments
Investments are recorded at market value.

Artworks
The artworks consist of items distributed to the Foundation by the Estate of Andy Warhol (the "Estate"). The Foundation recorded all artworks received from the Estate at their fair market value at the date of receipt as determined by independent appraisers.

Office furnishings, equipment and leasehold improvements
The cost of office furnishings, equipment and leasehold improvements is charged to expense when incurred because the Foundation does not deem such expenditures to be sufficiently material to warrant capitalization and depreciation or amortization.

Grants authorized
Grants, which are subject to routine performance requirements by the grantee, are treated as expenses at the time each individual grant is authorized by the Board of Directors. These grants are payable to the grantee according to the terms established by the Board of Directors.

Fair value of financial instruments
The Foundation's financial instruments consist of cash and

investments. The carrying amounts of cash and cash equivalents reported in the statement of financial position approximate fair value due to the short maturities of those instruments. The fair value of stocks, bonds and notes and mutual funds is based on publicly quoted market prices for those investments. The values of the limited equity partnerships and Alternative Investments adjusted for unrealized gains and losses, are based upon the most recent available information provided by management of the limited partnerships and alternative investments and may differ from the value that would have been used had a ready market for these investments existed. The Foundation believes that the fair value of all financial instruments as of April 30, 2006 does not differ materially from the aggregate carrying values of its financial instruments recorded in the accompanying statement of financial position.

Concentration of credit risk

The Foundation's financial instruments are potentially exposed to concentrations of credit risk. The Foundation places its cash with what it believes to be quality financial institutions. The Foundation's investments consist of bonds and notes, common and preferred stocks, mutual funds, limited equity partnerships and Alternative Investments. The Foundation believes no significant concentration of credit risk exists with respect to its cash and investments given the diversity of its holdings and the care exercised in selection.

Use of estimates

The preparation of financial statements requires management to make estimates and assumptions that affect the amounts reported in the financial statements. Actual results could differ from these estimates.

Note 3 – Tax status

The Foundation is exempt from Federal income tax under Section 501(c)(3) and is classified as a private foundation under Section 509(a) of the Internal Revenue Code. As such, the Foundation is subject to Federal excise tax on its net investment income, which includes interest and dividends, net realized gains on the sale of investments, royalties and licensing fees.

Note 4 – Retirement plan

The Foundation maintains, through Diversified Investment Advisors, a 403(b) retirement plan for all eligible employees. The Foundation's contributions are determined annually based on a percentage of eligible annual compensation of the participants up to a maximum of 20 percent of such eligible annual compensation. These contributions are 100 percent vested immediately for the benefit of the participants. The cost of this plan, during the 2006 and 2005 fiscal years amounted to $396,220 and $351,928, respectively. In addition, the participants may voluntarily contribute to the plan up to limits established by the Internal Revenue Code.

Note 5 – Commitments

Art storage

The Foundation has an agreement, which expires April 30, 2007, to lease off-site warehouse space to store its artworks. The agreement requires a fixed monthly rent of $31,235 for the first year, $32,484 for the second year and $33,784 in the third and final year of the agreement.

Note 2 – Investments

The following is a summary of the Foundation's investments at April 30, 2006 and 2005:

	April 30, 2006		April 30,2005	
	Cost	Market	Cost	Market
Bonds and notes	$ 36,451,615	$ 35,812,058	$ 33,153,246	$ 33,592,757
Common and preferred stocks	21,221,642	24,799,926	9,136,888	10,187,622
Mutual funds	44,482,352	50,001,320	48,846,168	50,697,390
Limited equity partnerships and like investments	29,174,238	42,376,085	21,254,738	24,698,724
Alternative investments	20,194,729	28,419,539	20,212,419	24,009,965
Total	$ 151,524,576	$ 181,408,928	$ 132,603,459	$ 143,186,458

The Foundation may, at its option, renew the lease for an additional two-year period through April 30, 2009. The Foundation may cancel the lease upon six months' written notice. The Foundation has the right to sublet a portion of the space as outlined in the agreement. In connection with the lease, the Foundation paid a security deposit of $48,949 to the landlord. Lease expense in connection with this agreement totaled $389,813 and $374,820 during the 2006 and 2005 fiscal years, respectively.

Office space

During January 2004, the Foundation extended its office lease, which was to expire June 30, 2004, for an additional seven and a half year period through December 31, 2011. Under the terms of the lease extension, the Foundation is required to pay a fixed annual rent of $215,000, effective July 1, 2004 through June 30, 2009, and $241,875 effective July 1, 2009 through December 31, 2011. In addition to the base rent, the Foundation is required to pay its proportionate share of increases in certain operating costs of the landlord over specified base levels as outlined in the agreement. In connection with the lease, the Foundation paid a security deposit totaling $17,967.

Catalogue Raisonné

During January 1995, the Foundation entered into a joint venture to produce and publish the Andy Warhol Catalogue Raisonné. Any royalties from the sale of this compilation will be divided between the Foundation and the venture partner based on the percentage of expenses incurred on the project by each party. The Foundation's plan for the Catalogue Raisonné anticipated ultimately transferring the Foundation's responsibility for production to The Andy Warhol Museum within the Carnegie Institute. To assist in meeting the Museum's expenses on the project, the Foundation authorized a grant of $2,400,000 payable over 12 years.

On August 1, 2000, the Foundation and its venture partner entered into a publishing contract pursuant to which the joint venture agreed to produce, and the publisher agreed to publish, the Catalogue Raisonné in six volumes over a twelve-year period. The first volume was published in March 2002 and the second volume in July 2004.

At its June 2004 meeting, the Board of Directors of the Foundation determined that production would remain with the Foundation. Authorization for the $2,400,000 grant to The Andy Warhol Museum for this project was rescinded; this obligation was removed from the Foundation's books and records during the 2005 fiscal year and has been netted against grants authorized in the Statement of Activities.

During the year ended April 30, 2006, the Foundation expended $397,409 on the project, including payroll and related expenditures of $379,309 and $18,100 of administrative and general expenses. As of April 30, 2006, the Foundation has expended a total of $2,862,625 on this project.

Creative Capital

During January 1999, a new organization named Creative Capital was founded to support individual artists pursuing innovative approaches to form and content in the media, performance, visual presentation and emerging arts fields. The Foundation provided, and continues to provide, office space for the organization.

During December 2000, the Foundation's Board of Directors approved a $10,000,000 matching grant, payable on May 1, 2004, provided Creative Capital met certain requirements. During the 2003 fiscal year, the Foundation restructured its commitment and pledged $2,000,000 of the $10,000,000 as a direct grant of which $1,000,000 was paid in April 2004 and the other $1,000,000 was paid in May 2004. During both the 2005 and 2006 fiscal years, Creative Capital met the requirements necessary to receive the $1,000,000 grant from the Foundation. The remaining $6,000,000 of the original grant will be paid out evenly over a six-year period provided that Creative Capital continues to meet specific requirements.

Arts Writing Initiative

During October 2005, the Foundation authorized $3,000,000 for a three-year grant program to support writers and non-profit publications to further the field of arts writing (the "Initiative"). In connection therewith, during the 2006 fiscal year, the Foundation disbursed $450,000. The remaining $2,550,000 is reflected as grants authorized but unpaid on the statement of financial position as of April 30, 2006.

Employment and service agreements

The Foundation has a service agreement, which can be terminated by either party under certain circumstances, whereby it engages the services of a specific individual as an agent for the sale of Warhol paintings, portraits, sculptures and drawings.

The Foundation also has a service agreement, which expires September 30, 2006, with another individual as an exclusive agent to sell select Warhol photographs and prints as well as artwork done by other individuals that was held by Andy Warhol at the time of his death and transferred by the Estate to the Foundation.

The Foundation has an employment agreement with a key employee, which expires September 30, 2006. It is subject to automatic renewal as of October 1, 2006 and annually thereafter, unless the Board notifies said employee to the contrary no later than September 30th of the prior year.

The Andy Warhol Museum

During September 1989, the Foundation entered into an agreement (the "Agreement") to establish The Andy Warhol Museum (the "Museum") in Pittsburgh, Pennsylvania as a separate, discrete museum within the Carnegie Institute. The Museum reflects the life and work of Andy Warhol.

The Museum's ongoing programs include the preservation, conservation, exhibition and presentation of the works and archives of Andy Warhol, as well as education of the general public, scholars and critics with respect to Andy Warhol's work and the effect of his work on contemporary and succeeding generations of artists.

The Museum opened during May 1994. During October 1998, the Foundation transferred certain artworks to the Museum; archival and related materials had been transferred previously.

Under the terms of the Agreement, should the Agreement be terminated, the ownership and physical possession of the works and archives provided by the Foundation to the Museum shall be re-conveyed to the Foundation.

The Andy Warhol Estate

The Estate was closed during April 1999. However, the agreements between the Estate and the Foundation pursuant to which the Estate transferred to the Foundation all the assets of the Estate provided that the Foundation would refund transferred property to the Estate to the extent that assets otherwise available to the Estate are insufficient to pay expenses or claims. During the 2006 and 2005 fiscal years, the Foundation paid expenses totaling $1,515 and $1,636, respectively, relating to the Estate.

Independent Auditors' Report on Accompanying Information

The Board of Directors
The Andy Warhol Foundation
for the Visual Arts, Inc.

Our audit was made for the purpose of forming an opinion on the basic financial statements (modified cash basis) taken as a whole. The information on page 12 provides additional analysis, which is not a required part of the basic financial statements (modified cash basis). Such information has been subjected to the auditing procedures applied in our audit of the basic financial statements (modified cash basis) and, in our opinion, is fairly stated in all material respects in relation to the basic financial statements (modified cash basis) taken as a whole.

August 10, 2006

Functional Statement of Activities

(Modified Cash Basis)

For The Year Ended April 30, 2006

Revenue
- Interest and dividends
- Royalties and licensing fees
- Other
  - Total

Expenses
- Grants authorized
- Other expenses
  - Payroll and related expenses
  - Salaries and wages
    - Payroll taxes and benefits
  - Directors' fees
  - Professional fees
    - Legal fees
    - Accounting fees
  - Consulting fees
  - Curator fees and related expenses
    - Curator expenses
    - Conservation expenses
  - Appraisal fees
  - Insurance
  - Meetings and travel
  - Federal excise tax
  - Art storage and related expenses
    - Art storage fees
    - Art storage expenses
  - Office expenses
  - Licensing expense
  - Rent
  - Catalogue Raisonné
  - Other
    - Authentication expense
    - Outside computer services
    - Membership fees
    - Office equipment
    - Filing fees
    - Miscellaneous
      - Total administrative and general
      - Total expenses
    - Excess (deficiency) of revenue over expenses before other additions (deductions)

Other additions (deductions)
- Net gain on sale of investments
- Net unrealized gain on investments
- Investment advisory fees
- Net gain on sale of artwork
- Commissions on the sale of artwork
- Estate of Andy Warhol
  - **Increase (decrease) in unrestricted net assets**

Total	Admin. and General	Program Activities	Investment Activities	Artworks and Related Activities	Royalties and Licensing	Estate and Other Extra Ordinary Matters
$ 4,344,664	$ -	$ -	$ 4,344,664	$ -	$ -	$ -
2,173,707	-	-	-	-	2,173,707	-
47,656	-	1,000	39,877	-	-	6,779
6,566,027	-	1,000	4,384,541	-	2,173,707	6,779
9,619,280	-	9,619,280	-	-	-	-
1,992,324	70,297	745,516	107,191	721,744	334,388	13,188
904,502	31,914	338,460	48,664	327,667	151,810	5,987
151,667	7,583	45,500	22,750	45,500	30,334	-
174,620	24,125	5,456	762	34,042	110,235	-
137,686	13,768	27,537	41,306	34,422	20,653	-
36,376	-	27,325	-	9,051	-	-
52,753	-	-	-	52,753	-	-
344,350	-	-	-	344,350	-	-
4,744	-	-	-	4,744	-	-
212,276	3,320	10,479	8,524	182,212	7,450	291
209,337	8,645	118,616	1,623	43,375	37,078	-
184,000	-	-	125,120	-	58,880	-
389,813	-	-	-	389,813	-	-
19,914	-	-	-	19,914	-	-
181,784	23,412	67,828	5,998	53,751	29,995	800
11,521	-	-	-	-	11,521	-
223,212	22,321	86,038	7,610	68,181	38,047	1,015
18,100	-	18,100	-	-	-	-
54,293	-	-	-	54,293	-	-
75,315	7,532	15,063	26,360	18,828	7,532	-
32,221	3,223	12,420	1,098	9,842	5,492	146
30,045	3,005	11,581	1,024	9,177	5,121	137
1,500	1,500	-	-	-	-	-
1,069	-	-	1,069	-	-	-
5,443,422	220,645	1,529,919	399,099	2,423,659	848,536	21,564
15,062,702	220,645	11,149,199	399,099	2,423,659	848,536	21,564
(8,496,675)	(220,645)	(11,148,199)	3,985,442	(2,423,659)	1,325,171	(14,785)
4,192,109	-	-	4,192,109	-	-	-
19,301,353	-	-	19,301,353	-	-	-
(560,810)	-	-	(560,810)	-	-	-
16,251,949	-	-	16,251,949	-	-	-
(1,664,967)	-	-	-	(1,664,967)	-	-
(1,515)	-	-	-	-	-	(1,515)
$29,021,444	**$ (220,645)**	**$(11,148,199)**	**$26,918,094**	**$12,163,323**	**$ 1,325,171**	**$ (16,300)**

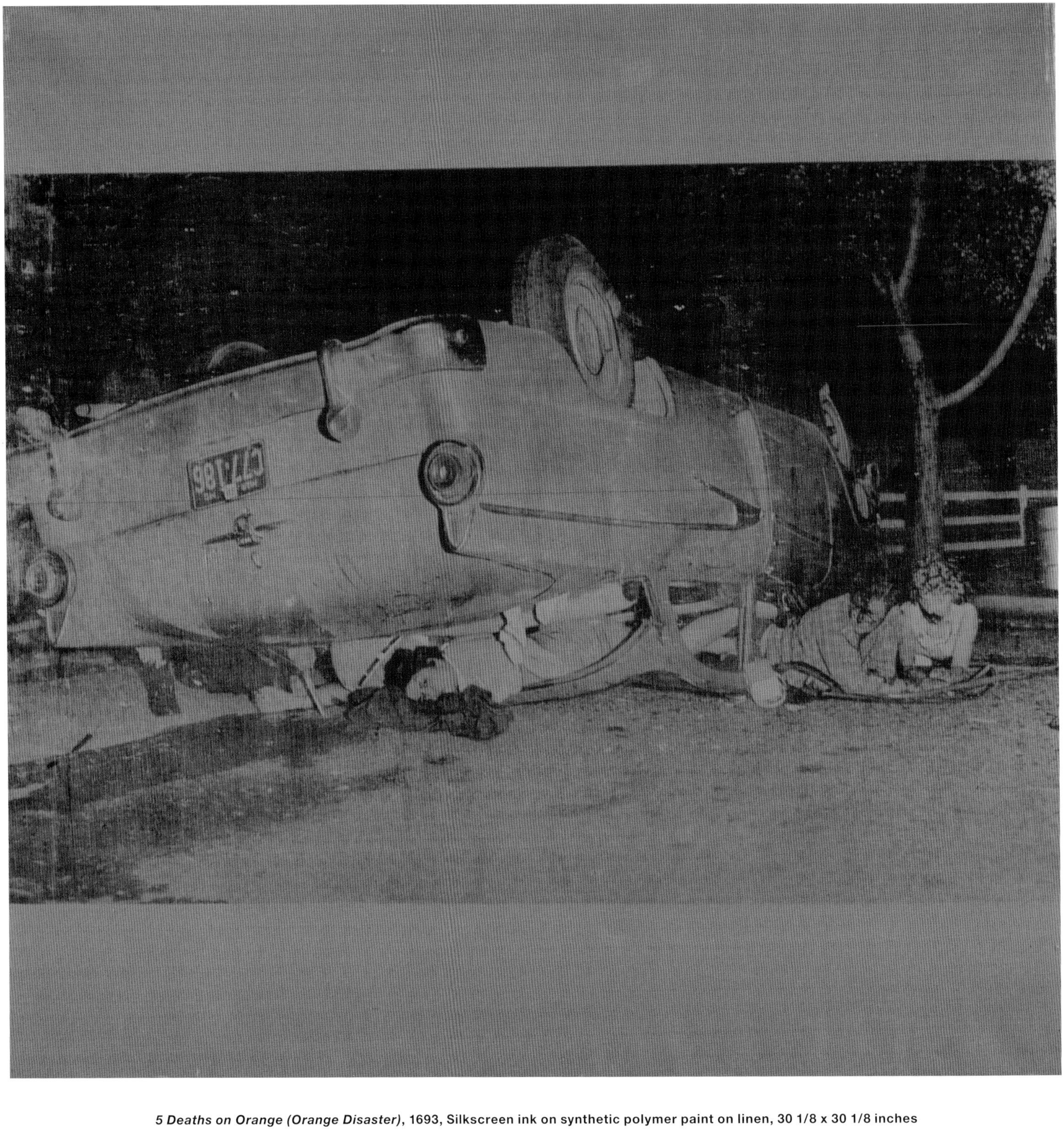

5 Deaths on Orange (Orange Disaster), 1693, Silkscreen ink on synthetic polymer paint on linen, 30 1/8 x 30 1/8 inches

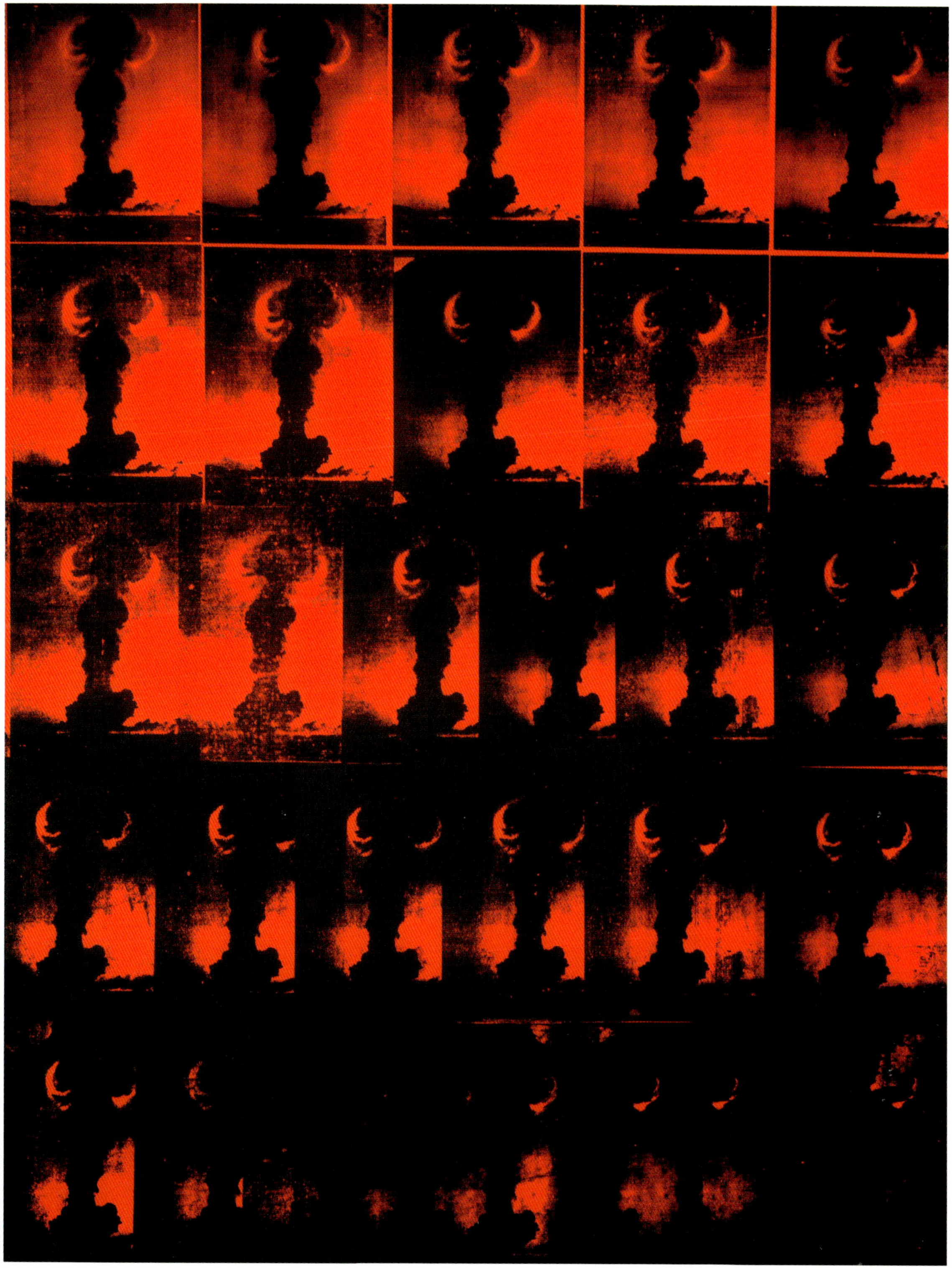

Red Explosion, 1963, Silkscreen ink and acrylic on linen, 103 3/4 x 80 1/4 inches

“The best time for me is when I don’t have any problems

that I can't buy my way out of."

Authentication Board

After Warhol's death on February 22, 1987 the Estate of Andy Warhol assumed initial responsibility for the authentication of works of art which were submitted for review by their owners. Fred Hughes, Executor, and subsequently Vincent Fremont, then Executive Manager, reviewed approximately 1,000 works between 1987 and 1995.

In May 1995, the foundation established the Andy Warhol Art Authentication Board, Inc. to continue to review the authenticity of works of art submitted by their owners. The Authentication Board is independent of the foundation and meets approximately three times a year to review submissions. Prior to review, the work is examined, researched, and thoroughly documented. After review, the owner receives a Letter of Opinion stating that, in the Board's opinion, the work is authentic (Exhibit A), not authentic (Exhibit B), or that the Board was unable to come to an opinion regarding the work (Exhibit C). The verso of the work is stamped accordingly. There is no charge to owners for this service. Since its inauguration in 1995, the Andy Warhol Art Authentication Board has reviewed approximately 4,000 works, including paintings, sculptures, drawings, prints and photographs.

The following have served as Directors of the Authentication Board: Jed Johnson, a long-time associate of Warhol (1995–1996); Robert Rosenblum, Professor of Fine Arts, New York University and Curator at the Solomon R. Guggenheim Museum (1996–2006); and David Whitney, an independent curator and founder of Factory Additions (1995–2005). The present Directors are Trevor Fairbrother, an independent scholar and curator (since 2005); Judith Goldman, a print historian and independent curator (since 2005); Sally King-Nero, Curator of Drawings and Photography at the Foundation and Executive Editor of the Andy Warhol Catalogue Raisonne (since 1997); and Neil Printz, Editor of the Andy Warhol Catalogue Raisonné (since 1995). Ronald D. Spencer, Esq. has served as the Authentication Board's legal counsel since 1996.

"We are indebted to the Foundation for understanding the challenges we face in presenting experimental works of art in the public realm." —*Creative Time, New York, NY*

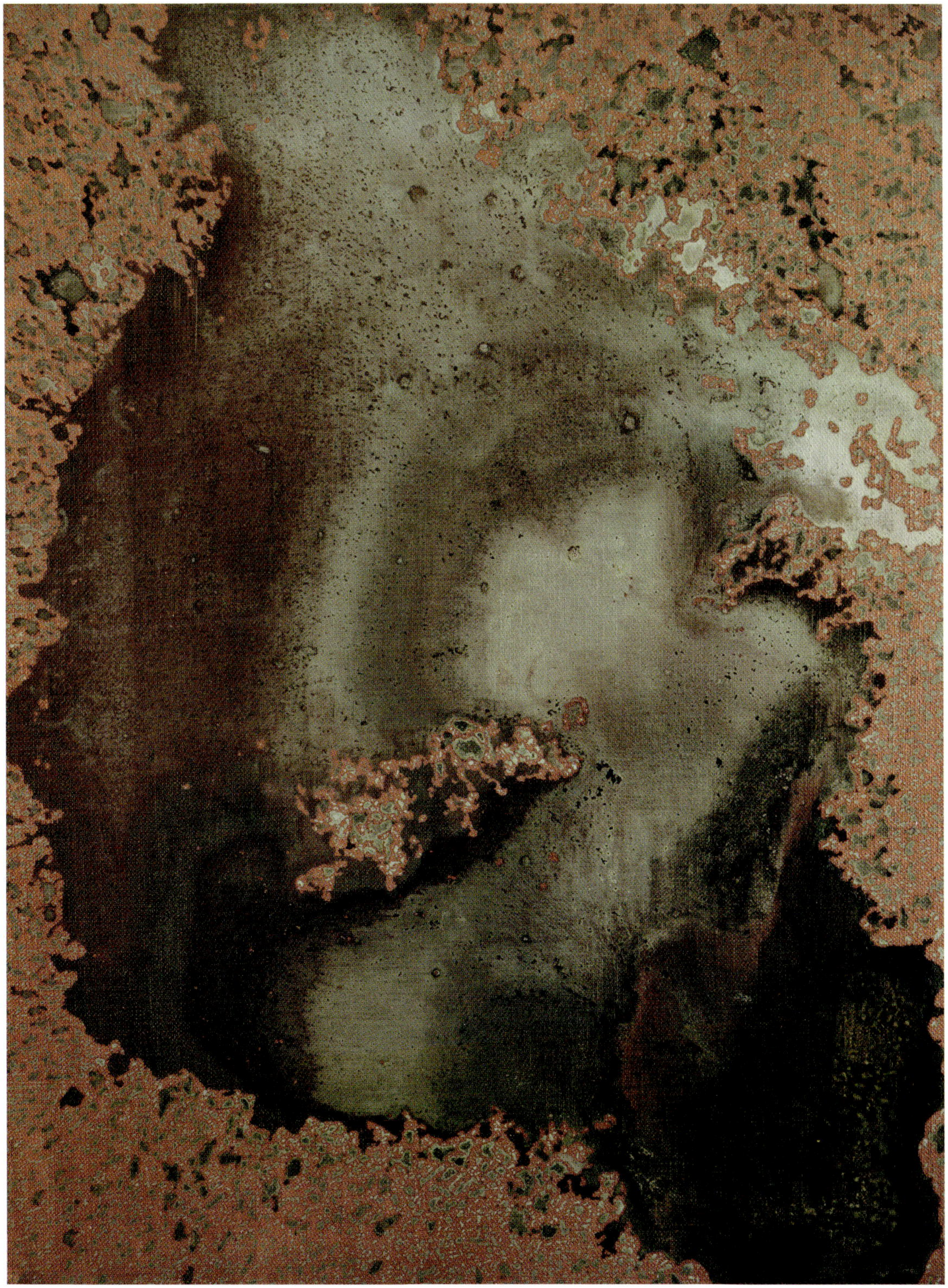

Oxidation Painting, 1978, Urine and metallic pigment in acrylic medium on canvas, 16 x 12 inches

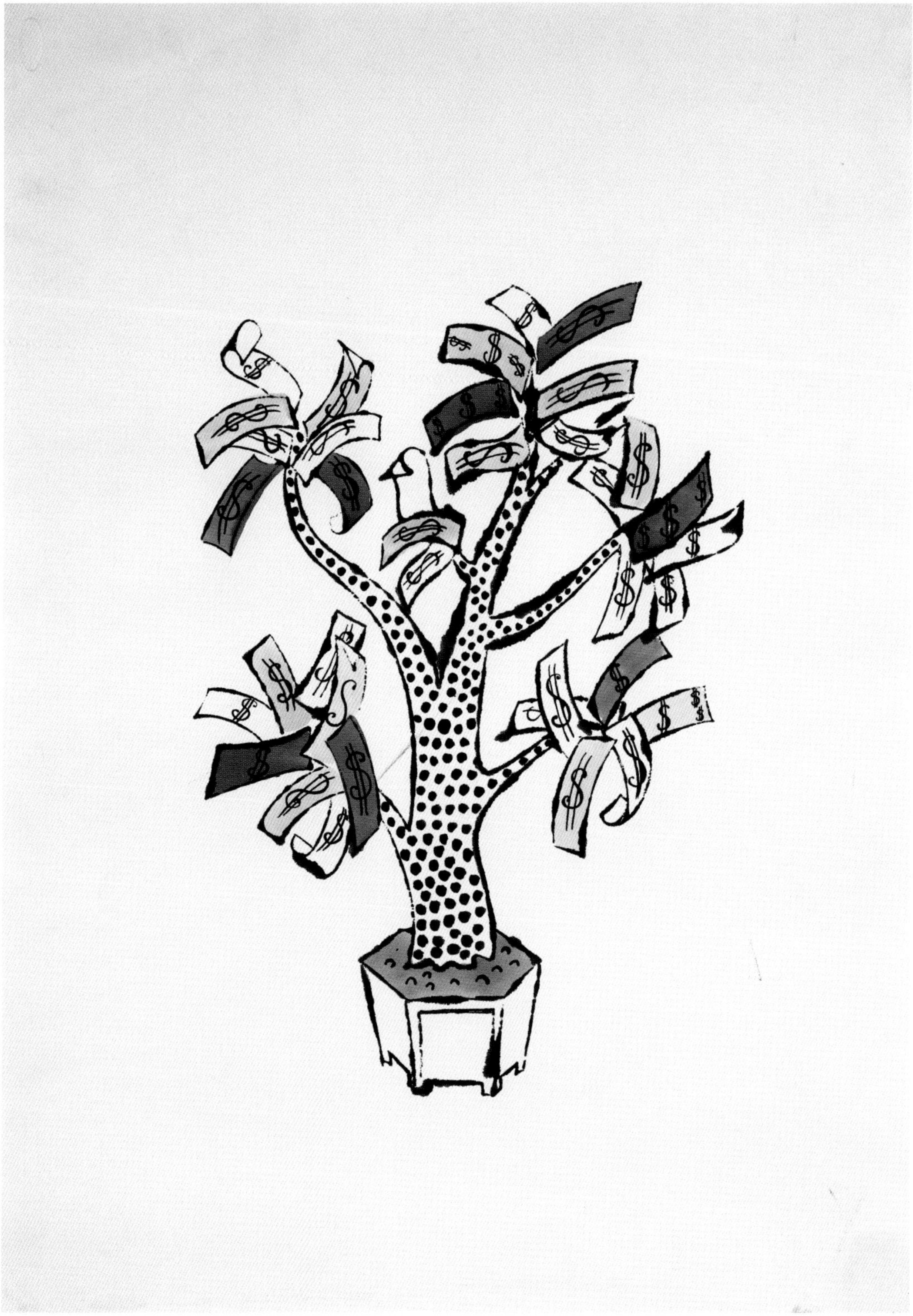

Money Tree, c.1957, Ink and wash on Strathmore paper, 22 1/2 x 16 1/2 inches

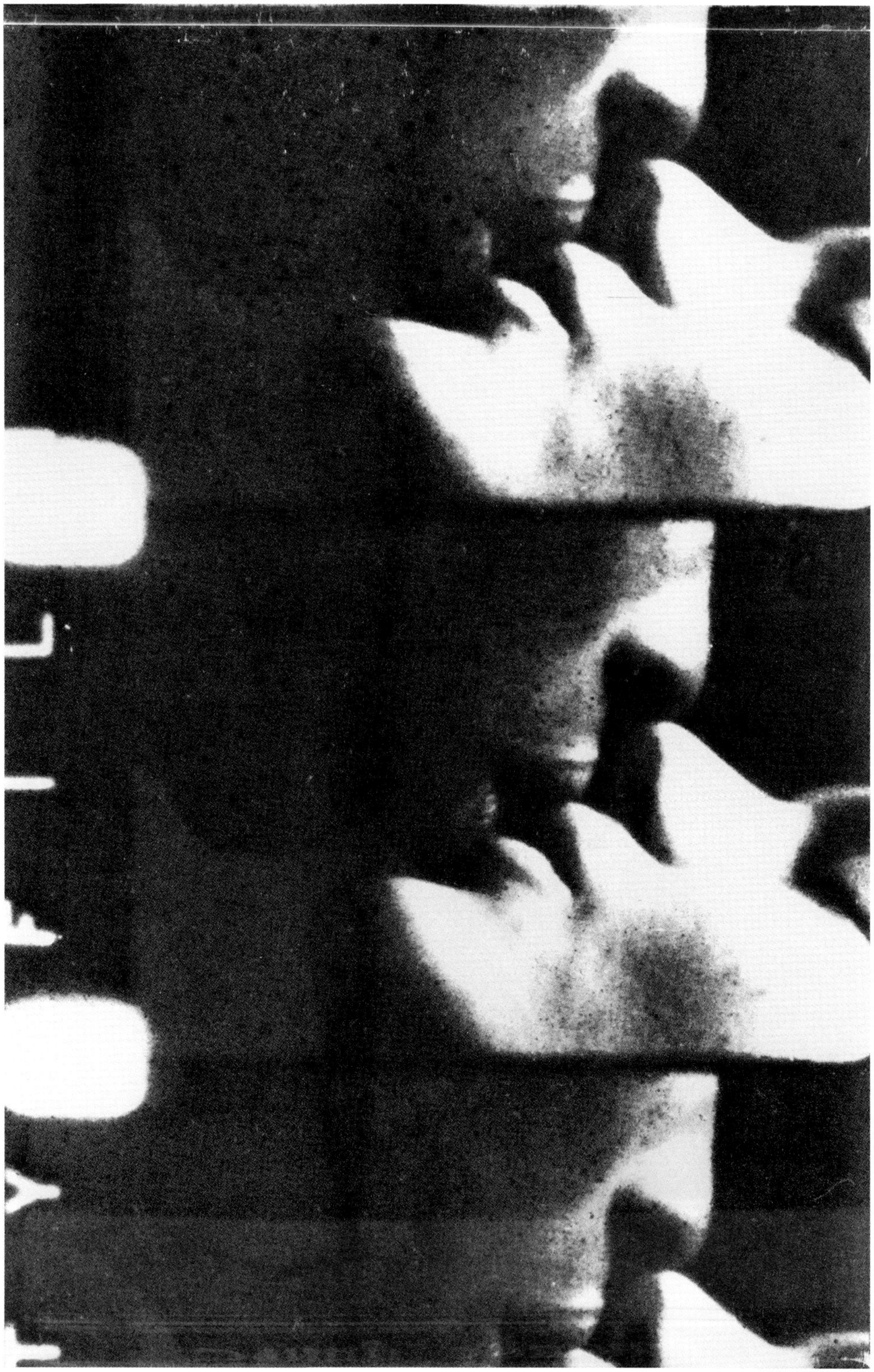

Kiss, 1966, Screen-print on plexiglas, 12 1/2 x 8 x 5 1/4 inches

“Everybody

must have a fantasy."

Board and Staff

Board of Directors and Officers

James Keith Brown
Patricia Cruz
David Dechman
Sherri Geldin, Chair
Jane Hammond
Rick Lowe
Ann R. Leven
Ann Philbin
Lisa Phillips
Jock Reynolds
Cindy Sherman
Michael Straus
Joel Wachs, President
Donald Warhola
John Waters
Patricia Williams
Robert G. Wilmers

KC Maurer, Treasurer
M. Antoinette Thomas, Secretary
John Warhola, Vice-President

Past Directors and Officers

Robert Denison
Vishakha N. Desai
Kinshasha Holman Conwill
Vincent Fremont
Brendan Gill, Past Chair
Archibald L. Gillies, Past President
Richard Gluckman
Agnes Gund
Kathy Halbreich
Frederick W. Hughes, Past Chair
Werner H. Kramarsky, Past Chair
Barbara Kruger
Susana Torruella Leval
Elizabeth Murray
Lord Palumbo
Anthony M. Solomon, Past Chair
Robert Storr
Charles B. Wright
John Warhola

Peter P. McN. Gates, Past Secretary

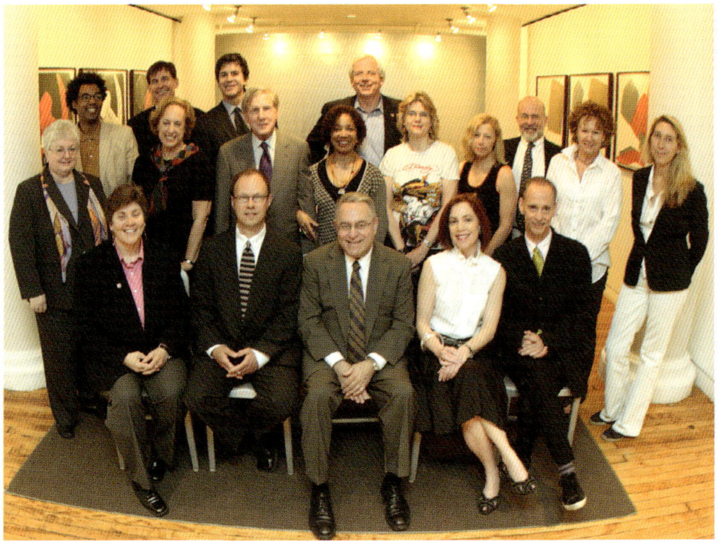

Staff

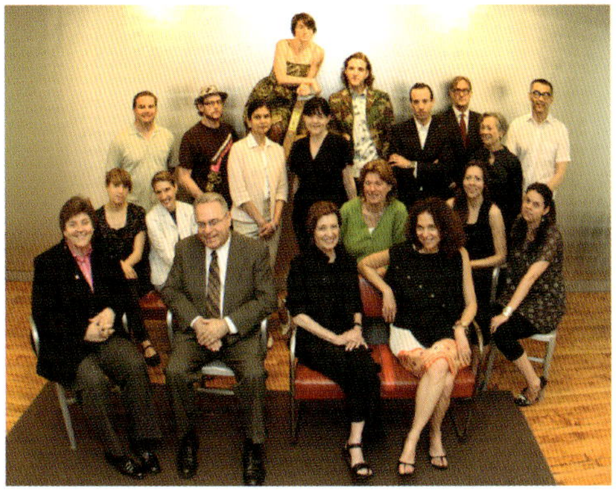

Yona Backer, Senior Program Officer
Vivienne Barriffe, Senior Accountant
Rachel Bers, Program Associate
Lauran Bonilla-Merchav, Research Assistant Catalogue Raisonné
Ken Chu, Collections Management
Pamela Clapp, Program Director
Lambert Corcoran, Collections Management
Julie Cummings, Office Manager
Pradeep Dalal, Program Associate, Creative Capital / Warhol Foundation Arts Writers' Grant Program
Claudia Defendi, Chief Curator, Curator of Prints, Co-Editor Catalogue Raisonné Prints, 3rd & 4th Editions
Nina Djerejian, Executive Assistant to the President
Jacqueline Farrell, Grants Administrator
Ben Fenton, Visual Resources Assistant, Andy Warhol Photographic Legacy Program
Scott Ferguson, Collections Management
Michael Hermann, Director of Licensing
Bibi Khan, Assistant Curator
Sally King-Nero, Curator of Drawings and Photography Executive Editor Catalogue Raisonné
Tomás Longo, Assistant Director of Licensing
KC Maurer, Chief Financial Officer
Jenny Moore, Project Curator, Andy Warhol Photographic Legacy Program
Deirdre O'Dwyer, Research and Curatorial Associate
Neil Printz, Editor Catalogue Raisonné
Beth Savage, Collections Coordinator
Margaret Sundell, Director, Creative Capital / Warhol Foundation Arts Writers' Grant Program
Anna Stein, Licensing Associate
Joel Wachs, President
John Warhola, Liaison to The Andy Warhol Museum

Past Staff

Brigid Berlin, Receptionist
David Bicknell, Collections Management
Victoria Binder, Research Assistant Catalogue Raisonné
Jennifer Brennan, Curatorial Assistant
Seth Bright, Program Assistant
Flordelino Bugarin, East 33rd Street Building Staff
Nenna Bugarin, East 64th Street House Staff
David Cabrera, Program Assistant
Carla Camacho, Research Assistant Catalogue Raisonné
Albert Ceslow, Montauk House Staff
Martin Cribbs, Director of Licensing
Valerie Chirigos, Assistant Curator, Photography
Eileen Clancy, Director, Andy Warhol Literary Properties
Mansita Diawara, Visual Resources Assistant, Andy Warhol Photographic Legacy Program
Pier Djerejian, Art Sales Coordinator
Jason Duval, Research and Curatorial Associate
Aurora Ferrer, East 64th Street House Staff
William Ganis, Visual Resources Assistant
Heloise Goodman, Administrative Assistant, Art Sales
Carol Greenberg, Secretary to the President
Rachel Gugelberger, Research Assistant Catalogue Raisonné
Ryan Humphrey, Collections Management
Terry Irwin, Coordinator, Film and Video Program
Jennifer Landey, Assistant to the Chair
Tomé Lazaro, East 33rd Street Building Superintendent
George Maley, East 33rd Street Building Staff
Lara Marcon, Assistant to the President
James McCauley, Comptroller, Licensing Manager
Timothy Mennel, Publishing Coordinator Catalogue Raisonné
Dara Meyers-Kingsley, Director, Film and Video Program
Matthew Miller, Collections Management
Karen Molleson, Curator
Sophia Padnos, Program Associate
Ruby Palmer, Office Manager
J. Scott Riker, Collections Management
Jane Rubin, Administrator of Collections
Ann Sass, Curator
Rosanne Sasso, Grants Administrator, Information Systems Manager
Sherle Schwenninger, Arts, Culture & Society Project Consultant
Jay Shriver, Collections Management
Kate Siplon, Assistant to the President, Information Systems Manager
Emily Todd, Program Director
Priya Wadhera, Research Assistant Catalogue Raisonné

Contributors: Rachel Bers, Claudia Defendi, Michael Hermann,
Jenny Moore, Sophia Padnos, Neil Printz
Editor: Rachel Bers
Image Research: Anna Stein
Design: Claudia Brandenburg, Language Arts, NY

Quotations from Andy Warhol: pages 4–5, 12–13, 24–25, 30–31,
40–41, 48–49, 56–57, 64–65, 70–71, 84–85, 90–91

Additional Credit Information:
p.17 Photo credit: Brian Forrest
p.18 Photo credit: Project Row Houses
p.33 (upper left) Photo credit: Christopher Burke
p.33 (upper right) Photo credit: Richard Stoner
p.33 (lower left) Photo credit: Zindman/Fremont
p.33 (lower right) Photo credit: Adam Reich
p.36 (top) Digital image photo credit: The Museum of Modern Art/
Licensed by SCALA / Art Resource, NY
p.36 (bottom) Digital image photo credit: The Museum of Modern
Art/Licensed by SCALA / Art Resource, NY
p.52 (top) Photo credit: Richard Stoner
p.52 (bottom) Photo credit: Richard Stoner
p.60 (upper right, lower left) Photographs by Kazutaka Nakamura
© Eyescream
p.92 Photo © Kate Milford
p.93 Photo © Kate Milford

covers: *Sunset*, 1972, Screen-print on white paper, 34 x 34 inches